A Story to Tell

Edited by George Murphy
and Maggie Power

Trentham Books

Stoke on Trent, UK and Sterling, USA

Trentham Books Limited
Westview House   22883 Quicksilver Drive
734 London Road   Sterling
Oakhill   VA 20166-2012
Stoke on Trent   USA
Staffordshire
England ST4 5NP

First published 2009

British Library Cataloguing-in-Publication Data
A catalogue record for this book is available from the British Library

ISBN: 978 1 85856 443 2

Cover photograph: a child listening to a story at Dryclough Infant School, Huddersfield.

Designed and typeset by Trentham Print Design Ltd, Chester and printed in Great Britain by Cpod, Trowbridge, Wiltshire.

Contents

Preface

A story to tell
Why this book?
And why now?

Jack Zipes wrote

> Schools are always in a state of transition or crisis. In every city or country in
> which I have worked, the demands placed on schools and teachers are
> enormous because the public perceives that 'they' are failing our children. In
> response school administrators and teachers, who are under great stress,
> sometimes react defensively to teachers and governments who provide little
> support and few initiatives to improve the conditions under which teachers
> labour. – and they often labour with great frustration instead of having time to
> experiment with innovative teaching methods.

Zipes went on to argue for storytellers working in schools to help instil a sense
of community, to demonstrate how 'the ordinary can become the extraordinary'. He was writing in 1995 but surely his words apply to us here and now.

We believe they do. We are finding that some of the constraints on schools
and teachers in the UK have loosened just a little. We know the benefits that
can come from letting the story into the classroom.

We believe that story can refer to both the personal and that which exists in
our communities and we feel the importance of writing about both.

Why this book?

We have worked with our many contributors to enable them to talk, sometimes of the place of story in their own lives but always to outline the importance of working with narrative in the primary classroom.

Acknowledgements

We wish to thank all those who have helped us in the preparation of this book, especially of course the contributors.

George would also like to acknowledge the support and patience of his wife Kate, his daughter Leah – who still laughs in the right places at his stories – and his son Jude for being a cool dude and brave with it. Thanks are also due to students on the storytelling modules and to the Registered Teachers and B.Ed students for help with research. Finally, he thanks his colleagues and managers at Bradford College for their patient support over the past twelve months.

Maggie would in addition like to thank colleagues past and present who have helped her to grow as a story maker. It all started with the inspirational Storybox project and Norah McWilliam. That made a difference to so many as did the work and wisdom of Inge Cramer who has been yet again a valuable friend and critic with this endeavour as in so many others.

She would also like to thank her special story makers, Chris, Anna and Laura.

It has been agreed that profits from this book will be donated to charity – to Book Aid International, which supports literature, education and development in sub-Saharan Africa.

Contributors

George Murphy is a senior lecturer at Bradford College. He has written several books for children based on adaptations of traditional folktales.

Maggie Power is a senior lecturer at Bradford College. As well as writing on language and humanities she is well known for her storytelling performances in schools.

Monica Best is a graduate of Bradford College and teaches in Huddersfield.

Kate Cleary is a senior lecturer at Bradford College and a former advisory teacher for history.

Sally Greenwood is a graduate of Bradford College and teaches in Bradford.

Wendy Holland is an early years' and language specialist and a senior lecturer at Bradford College.

David Jones is headteacher of a Bradford primary school.

Shabana Kausar is a graduate from the Education Studies course at Bradford College where she is completing the post graduate certificate of education course.

Howard Lisle is a senior lecturer at Bradford College and has acted as the BBC advisor for primary geography at Key Stage 2.

Christine McMahon is a restorative justice officer and professional storyteller based in Hebden Bridge, West Yorkshire

Caroline Moore is lay chaplain at Bradford Cathedral, where she is involved in educational work.

Clare Muireann Murphy is a professional storyteller based in Galway.

Christine Seton is a primary school teacher in Calderdale.

Introduction
Our Stories

In the introduction to her book of fairy tales, Angela Carter writes,

> For most of human history, 'literature', both fiction and poetry, has been narrated, heard, not read. So fairy tales, folktales, stories from the oral tradition are the most vital connection we have with the imaginations of the ordinary men and women whose labour created our world. (1990)

We want to take you on a journey that will look at the role and place of narrative in the primary classroom. Before we do, we want to share a little of our own stories with you. How have we reached the position we are in today? What has brought each of us to value story so highly and place it at the heart of the education of children?

George's story

Some of my favourite memories of infant school are the afternoons when white-haired Miss Jones unlocked the book cupboard and told us that we could rest our heads on our desks and listen to a story. *The Magic Faraway Tree* easily transported her class of 42 infants to a world brimming with more possibilities than the dreary confines of Ellesmere Port in the 1950s.

Very rarely did our teachers shut the book and tell us a story directly. We were too young for wartime reminiscences of brothers or beaus who went off to fight but never returned, or for tragic and stirring tales of the Merseyside blitz. Everyone has personal anecdotes and tales that they jazz up and adapt for different audiences. But our teachers never shared their family tales with us and they never asked us for ours.

In my second year at school we'd had a young, newly qualified teacher called Miss Kopak, who looked like a younger version of Sylvia Appleyard (a television presenter who told stories on *Watch with mother*). Miss Kopak allowed us to get out from behind our desks in the afternoons to play in the sand tray or the Wendy House. And afterwards, she would sit us around her on tiny chairs and read to us from a storybook with pictures in. Or sometimes she would tell us a tale. The ancient spell she conjured up is what this book is about: teller and audience without the authored text between them, each reacting to the other, sharing an experience but each one seeing their own imagined tale.

The girls especially liked *Goldilocks and the Three Bears*, with its clever ratcheting up of tension and the spoken bits when we all joined in. As listeners we shared a secret knowledge and the excitement never failed to mount as we waited for the sleeping girl to be discovered.

Even more thrilling was *Red Riding Hood*. The strangeness of a heroine who couldn't distinguish between a granny and a wolf in a petticoat only enhanced our enjoyment as we joined in with their dialogue. The recovery of the slightly distressed, but not too badly damaged, old woman from the wolf's belly only added to the story's fascination.

But the story I liked best was *Jack and the Beanstalk*. As with *The Magic Faraway Tree* the story took us to a different world beyond the clouds. I always felt sorry for the ogre's wife; mealtimes must have been very demanding and she was stern but kind to Jack. But the ogre was satisfyingly bad enough not to worry too much about Jack's appropriation of his property. Best of all, the story had a good chase scene and I felt an affinity for a hero who was famous for getting things wrong.

I once read a student's retelling of this tale in which Jack and the ogre become friends. Done sharply, these satirical retellings can work well. In a similar reworking, I've seen a troll threatened with an ASBO, after complaints from neighbouring goats, before agreeing to undertake anger management training. In this case, the ogre embraced vegetarianism and shared his wealth with Jack's family. This sorted out the social situation but killed the story. Whatever else happens you have to keep the 'Fee Fi Foh Fum!'

A few years ago, I wrote a picture book version of *Jack and the Beanstalk* in a series for African children. The editors persuaded me to omit my chorus of 'Fee Fi Foh Fum! I smell the blood of a farmer's son. Be he alive or be he dead, I'll grind his bones to make my bread!' It was changed to: 'Fee Fi Foh Fum! I want to eat the little boy!

This retains the basic message, but I think the chorus loses something.

My other early memories of storytelling are the tales told by my father. My dad suffered from something called 'blood pressure' that made all our lives a misery. Most evenings my sisters and I would lie awake and listen to our parents rowing. But sometimes, when he came home early from the Cheshire Cat, with a bottle of Mackeson for my mum and crisps and pop for us, we turned the TV off and played Newmarket or Sevens and dad sang 'I'll take you home again, Kathleen' to my sister Kath. And he told us his wartime stories.

Dad's war stories were always humorous. There was one about a soldier who asked for leave because he was deaf. The doctor played along with this until the soldier was about to exit, when the doctor whispered 'Shut the door please, private'. The private duly complied before realising his mistake. What was funnier than the story was the way dad always laughed at its conclusion.

He told a story about an incident when he was disembarked for the first time onto the dock in India with thousands of other squaddies. The order was given to send a tea urn around the troops to give every man a drink. When my dad's turn came he asked the sergeant, very politely, 'Can I have my tea without sugar, sergeant?'

We squirmed every time he told this tale and imagined Dad's embarrassment as the bellowing sergeant drew the attention of the massed ranks to his request. It was thirty years later that my wife heard the same story on a Radio 4 programme about apocryphal tales.

When our parents divorced, my dad moved south, remarried and got a job as a Commissionaire at the BBC in London. The last time I saw him before he died he complied with my requests and told me some terrible, true stories about the war. He asked me if I could get hold of his medals, especially the Burma Star. I said I would see what I could do, knowing that my mum had thrown them all away on the same day that she cut him out of our family photographs.

The instinct *not* to tell personal tales was even more ingrained in my mother. Born and bred in Ellesmere Port, her family originating from the Welsh borders, she lacked my dad's Scouse loquaciousness and his bad temper. One day she was washing up and started to sing the old music hall song, 'Someone's in the kitchen with Dinah'. She stopped suddenly and confided to my youngest sister that she once had a sister called Dinah, who died in her teens. Then mum went back to her washing up. My sister Chris was in her mid-teens by then and it was the first and only time any of us heard about our Aunty Dinah.

After mum's death we discovered we had an Uncle Norman we had never been told about. As a baby he had been given away to another couple because they couldn't have children and our mum's family had too many. We realised that we had grown up and gone to school with his children and never known that they were our cousins.

But it was 1989 before I saw someone who spoke up for oral storytelling in classrooms, for the retelling of traditional tales and for tapping into the stories families tell about themselves. I attended a Storytelling session given by Betty Rosen.

Betty had worked in a tough secondary school in Tottenham and used Greek myths and folktales as a stimulus for her pupils' own storytelling and writing. The first task she gave us was to tell about our first memories. I found I could dredge up bits of anecdotes I had told to family and friends – some of which I had worked up into little bits of written stories. Under pressure to produce something, I suddenly found that I could knit them together into a single tale.

Betty told us some of her favourite tales and she set us to write a version of the Irish myth of *Tir Nan Og*. We could retell it in our own words or we could change it. I found that having the support of an ancient story allowed me to write a rejoinder. My hero returned from a land without want and sorrow, where time stood still, to the Ireland of the troubles, drawn back by the prayers of his people who wouldn't let their history rest nor look to the future. We all contributed our tales and Betty included them in *Shapers and Polishers* (1991).

During the next few years I was able to tell traditional tales in a range of primary and secondary schools. Sometimes I used them to support pupils' own storytelling and sometimes as a prompt for writing. Traditional tales are the best resource I have ever found for scaffolding children's attempts at oral and written narratives. I found that a good introduction was to share and elicit personal tales.

At Bradford College I teach a *Traditional Tales* module – developed by colleagues over the past decade – to prospective teachers and educationists. I have recently joined the Shaggy Dog Storytellers club and once a month I experience again the mesmerising power of personal and ancient tales told by professional and amateur performers.

Maggie's story

The first six years of my life were spent in Ireland, in a small town on the coast, just below the border with the north. The third of four children, life was busy for all of us and it is not so much that I can remember quiet story times but more that stories were in the air; we were a family of talkers and tellers. If anything, I was more the listener, the quiet one then but I do remember the use of stories, the big dolls' house that I turned on its side, climbed into and where I spent hours sailing off to other places, the new shoes that I let sail away while I waved goodbye to the boats and wished them well as they were carried away on the tide.

It was a forced and rushed move to England after my father, who was working between England and Ireland, had a heart attack. We needed to be together and a cousin's house was available to rent. It was a hard time, especially for my mother and older brother and sister who had to leave so much more behind. And then the long journey, first to Dublin, then the boat to Wales and then a long train ride to London.

It was made more stressful for all by the story that at that time was in my head. I wouldn't get off the boat. I didn't want to go to England. I dearly wanted to be with my adored father but not to stand on English soil – It was St Patrick: you know he had cast all the snakes out of Ireland and in my little head that meant they had all swum to England and I didn't want to be bitten by one. Who told me the story? I don't remember, but it was one of many in my head.

School at first meant being quiet, as I sounded so different and was very much an outsider ... but there were stories at the end of each day and play time became the time to build a castle of benches and enter a world of princesses and dragons, and gallop around, on and on. The school was a long way from home; we lived near the southern end of the Northern line, just outside Morden and the school was in Wimbledon, a convent school in beautiful grounds that gave space and opportunity. I remember stories and rhymes, those we chanted about Miss Potter being a rotter and wasn't it time we shot her. But always the stories were told at the end of the day. And from very early on in that little school I remember thinking I wanted to be that teacher, I wanted to talk to and tell stories to children, and to help them read and write and to tell them stories at the end of the day. My main concern was that I would be unable to spell all the names on the register as there were many children of Polish and Italian heritage, with long names.

My father recovered from his first heart attack and did not die until I was twenty and nearly qualified as that teacher. Along the way I had been enriched by some very good teachers. Mrs Flanagan in particular, who floated us in a sea of stories, took us on the journey into new and different worlds of tales. I also did an O level in Greek Literature in translation, which took me into a new and very different world and make me realise the ancient and essential nature of tales and telling.

But even more important were the times at home, the Sunday lunches that went on long into the afternoon as we outdid each other with stories one after another – the crack, as they say, was good ... and best of all was my father's ability to weave a tale about past exploits or folk or times long gone. The stories were rich and varied but in some ways left me with a confused identity. I had an identity that located me elsewhere but a presence in a country that we had been forced into for economic reasons. I believe that this experience helped me later to relate to families and children who had also moved across and between lands.

My first teaching was as a volunteer in Africa, in Tanzania. A primary school teacher who had specialised in English and Drama, I was dropped into a large school in Dar es Salaam. Some of the older students had themselves been teaching but needed to go to secondary school to upgrade their qualifications. All rather intimidating.

I needed to discover the rich stories that came from the different regions and learn them fast. We did have the visiting British Council Landrover that unrolled a screen and showed us films of Shakespeare in the African night but we had to study the works on Ngugi, Achebe and other African writers.

Back in London two years later, I got a job teaching in a secondary modern school in South London. It was the London Borough of Sutton and they had a number of grammar schools but, if my memory serves me right, only one comprehensive and some secondary moderns. I loved it and soon learned that the way to capture the attention of most pupils was through a tale.

With a team of others we were able to put on plays and musicals that offered so much to so many. But there were challenges. When we did *Oliver* I had to persuade the senior management not to suspend a child who had been arrested for shoplifting. Had I not succeeded I would have been without my Fagin: 'You told me to practise Miss' ... 'But I meant the words, Christopher.'

The power of entering into a tale was important but one of my strongest memories was to do with a production of *The Match Girls* by Bill Owen. We had the story of the girls who became ill and died, many after developing 'phossie jaw' from the chemicals. There was more freedom then, less constraint even on secondary schools in what could be covered in the curriculum. We took the children into central London. We were allowed to visit the archives of the match company, which was still in existence, and to read and study the lives of the workers. It was as though they were with us as they told their stories of struggle, work, illness and loss. The girls wrote their own stories as Matchgirls and we had a production that I know lives on in many of us. We had linked to and captured the stories of people of another era.

Marriage, family and moving north gave me space and time to tell and share stories with my two young daughters. They have both retained a love and passion for tales. They remember certain special tales among them *Dogger* by Shirley Hughes. Her work stayed with us. On a recent visit to Oxford we gazed at Dogger himself, sitting in a showcase, ear to the side, alongside the original artwork. We had all walked past the various works on display to feast our eyes on the realisation of this little dog.

At home there were stories every night. I remember the struggle to finish sometimes when my second baby needed attention but she had to wait while the story was finished. Imagination is all; I also remember a lipstick being used to cover the baby in red. 'It's ok mummy. I have made her into a red Alien, like the one in the story last night'. The children lived in dressing up clothes.

The plays and the stories happened at even the most inconvenient times. But of particular importance to both girls were the stories that were told on long car rides to visit relatives. Their father has, as we say, a way with words, and while he drove he would captivate them with tales about animals.

I began working in a primary school in Bradford, using story and drama to bring on the children's language development. And again there were stories to tell and act out, but now we needed to look at Akhbar and not just at the supposedly European tales. In a way I had come full circle. I was once more with families who had moved and who needed to feel that the school knew and acknowledged this. We had to ensure that the history, culture and faith of the children could come into school.

One of the most memorable projects I worked on in the many years I was at the school focused on collecting the stories of people's journeys to Bradford. We started with the staff and then went out with a video camera and listened. And there was so much to listen to: stories of young men who had fought with the British in the Second World War and been encouraged to come to Bradford, stories of fathers who had come from Afghanistan to study and had to journey back via Pakistan to rescue and bring out family members during the war with Russia. We brought the narrative into school. We had a history that was alive and relevant, in which the children could see themselves and their journey as being important and valued. They had stories to collect and tell and we wanted to listen.

But that was before the drilling and testing regime became so entrenched in schools. Some of us believed that education as we practised it was truly about empowerment – and I believe it worked. I do not have the statistics – that would be another book – but I do know that many of those children are now gainfully employed and that some are teachers. Working in the college where I do now, there are always some students each year who come up to me and say, 'Miss, do you remember when ... we told that story ... we talked to grannies'.

We needed to have the time to tell stories, to give stories to children. One of my most cherished memories is of sharing a story with a class of six year olds and asking them to take the story home and tell it to someone that day. (It was part of a linked European project where stories were being told and collected.) But what stays with me as an abiding memory is of this little boy standing in line and getting ready to leave the room. He had his hands pushed against his ears. 'What are you doing?' I asked. 'I am keeping it in ... the story ... I want it to stay in my head until I get home'.

Working with narrative is about telling and listening and we need to develop the need to do both in a relevant and creative way.

Part 1
**Storytelling –
Language and Literature**

Storytelling in primary schools
George Murphy

In this chapter, George looks at the place of oral storytelling in language and literacy teaching. He considers the practical issues: where to find the right stories; how to support retelling and rewriting tales; how to examine different types of stories in language and literacy sessions. Finally, he argues for the place of personal tales and suggests ways of managing the transition to telling traditional stories.

Storytelling in schools

Oral storytelling and the spoken or written retelling of traditional tales has never completely disappeared from primary school practice. Fairytales have long been read and – sometimes – told in early years' classrooms. However, the engagement with a more diverse range of folktales, myths and legends is now widespread. When we first got the idea for this book we thought it would be useful to check the level of storytelling activity in schools in our local area, as we thought that this might give us an idea of the national picture. We asked some of Bradford's primary language and literacy advisers if they knew of any schools that were using oral storytelling as part of the English curriculum. They knew of three schools that had recently held training days with talks by a visiting storyteller. Teachers visiting us in college have mentioned Pie Corbett's work approvingly. His *Bumper Book of Story-telling into Writing* (2006) offers practical advice on learning tales, performing tales, changing and adding to tales. In neighbouring Calderdale, the Shaggy-dog Storytellers club worked with schools in the upper valley during 2007 and 2008 on the Arts Council funded Todmorden Touchwood project.

Storytelling in schools may well become more popular. In our area this is partly due to the influence of the Traditional Tales module developed by colleagues over the last decade. When we contacted former students we found that several had remained interested in various aspects of storytelling, retelling and rewriting tales. Examples of their classroom work appear in this book. I discovered that Hebden Bridge storyteller Christine McMahon had attended the Narrative Studies evening class at the college and remembers visiting the library and reading the collections of Katherine Briggs with great pleasure. She told me: 'I've still got my essay!' The Traditional Tales module now includes an assessed performance alongside the theoretical and written aspects.

No doubt other regions would show a similar pattern of storytelling, driven forward by enthusiasts and development programmes. For the country as a whole, the use of traditional tales has been boosted by its presence in curriculum guidance documents. Pick up the *Primary Framework for Literacy and Mathematics* (2006) and you'll find a succession of targets for the use of spoken stories. At the Foundation Stage, most children are expected to: 'Retell narratives in the correct sequence, drawing on the language patterns of stories' (p23).

By year 5 a core learning goal states that children should: 'Tell a story using notes designed to cue techniques, such as repetition, recap and humour' (p23). There is less explicit attention to personal stories, although in year 1 most children should: 'Tell stories and describe incidents from their own experience in an audible voice' (p40).

Whilst we have been gathering examples of practice for this volume we have found that the *Primary Framework* has acted as a spur for storytelling to be written into yearly planning. But we sometimes worry lest the learning goals distort genuine engagement with traditional stories. Teachers can sometimes confuse the worthy idea of children learning to retell favourite stories with a desire to drill children towards verbatim recall. The goal of children 'using the conventions of familiar storytelling language' can be reduced in practice to a teacher ticking a list of interesting (but memorised) connectives. This is one of the problems with behavioural objectives. Teachers are asked to achieve a measurable learning target with a group of children. The targets might be laudable in themselves and children can learn a great deal from genre-switching and other activities, but the long term and affective aspects of literacy work can be overlooked.

This was one of the criticisms of Literacy Hour practice. I have seen a teacher in a literacy hour session project onto the whiteboard an early 19th century prayer by a North American Indian, a prayer addressed to the god of nature, asking him for protection from the ravages of white settlers. It was a very powerful piece, but the teacher's first follow up question was, 'Can you find the adjectives in this text?'

Now, certainly, attention to vocabulary and linguistic techniques is important. Handled correctly, word and sentence level activities can help children to understand how powerful writing is constructed. On this occasion, however, I felt that the teacher was losing sight of larger issues, perhaps because they didn't appear in her set of literacy learning objectives. As more attention is turned to traditional and personal storytelling, I hope that teachers do not lose their focus on long term aims when planning to hit short range targets.

Finding the right tale to tell

Traditional tales can be categorised as myths and folktales – in all their varieties, but especially legends, nursery and fairy tales. When labelling spoken tales in terms of genre, folklorists often characterise them according to the way in which they were received by audiences rather than by their recurring structures (see, for example, Swales, 1990, p35). In this analysis, narratives that were regarded as sacred are labelled as myths. Tales that can be seen as having some grounding in fact can be described as legends. We can connect individual myths to cycles of stories that reveal ancient belief systems, in particular parts of the world during specific historical periods. Myths give narrative answers to questions of creation and natural order; they concern the actions of gods and the impact of those actions on human beings.

Campbell (1993) and others have pointed out the recurring structures found in these ancient tales. The patterns discerned in hero tales have influenced the construction of *Star Wars* and other recent fictions. Without necessarily accepting that Campbell's psychoanalytical analysis of heroic quest tales from different times and places uncovers a universal archetype, it is clear that the survival of such myths is based on the great recurring themes of life and love and death that connect us all. Myths retain much of their power and sharing them with children should consist of more than a simple attention to narrative structure.

The term 'folktales' covers a vast array of narrative forms. The stories tend to be short. The focus is on action and often on the thwarted or rewarded aspirations of everyman. If you read through collections of folktales (perhaps

Briggs, 1977) you'll find categories such as Fables, Jocular tales, Black dogs, Bogies, Dragons, Fairies, Nursery tales, Ghosts, Giants. In these collected tales, although many categories are openly fantastical, others read more as recounts of events, with reference to specific local detail in an apparent attempt to prove their grounding in fact.

These tales were gathered from tellers who seem at times to be more concerned to convince the listener of the veracity of their tale than to spin an entertaining yarn, as in: 'This tale was told by one who knew all three men personally'. Many collections are based on regional rather than thematic classifications and anthologists have often tried to provide a bare representation of the key elements of tales – because oral retellings were never constant. These collections can provide raw material for teachers and children to examine local legends, for many tales seek to explain local phenomena. To what extent can they be considered the forerunners of today's UFO stories and the rural equivalent of our urban myths?

It is more likely, however, that you will turn first to some of the many anthologies of myths and folktales aimed at children and the general reader. In these collections, the authors will probably have taken out some of the archaic local and historical detail. Dialect usage will be controlled or contextualised to support the reader's understanding. If you find a tale you like, I suggest that you put it to one side until you can compare it to a different version. Then perhaps do some research to establish the provenance of your tale and see how it compares to similar stories from other cultures. Finally, create your own version, one that suits your audience. But don't lose sight of the flavour and distinctiveness that first attracted you to the tale. Make your listeners want to move into your world: don't feel that your story has to travel all the way into theirs.

I also suggest that you hear stories being told. Most told stories might not stay with you. But some will get into your blood stream. Stories were designed to infect people – and the infection is contagious, because you'll want to pass it on.

Some of the students at Bradford whose families have arrived in the UK in the last few decades can retell folktales their parents and grandparents told them when they were growing up. Schools can tap into this resource by inviting parents and elders to share the tales they were told when they were children. Equally, they can support children's retellings and teachers can record and support the learning of favourite tales by establishing a class anthology of tales from different parts of the world.

Retelling and rewriting

Reflecting on his approach to collecting and representing stories for his great anthology *Italian Folktales* (2000), Italo Calvino wrote,

> In all this I was guided by the Tuscan proverb ... *The tale is not beautiful if nothing is added to it* – in other words, its value consists in what is woven and rewoven into it; I have thought of myself as a link in the anonymous chain without end by which folktales are handed down, links that are never merely instruments or passive transmitters, but ... its real 'authors'. (pxxi)

It has been recognised for some time (see Perera, 1989) that children find it easier to make sense of information when it is ordered in a regular pattern – as with the chronological patterning of traditional tales. At its most straightforward, the folktale introduces character and setting, presents a challenge to the hero, and describes a series of events leading to a definitive resolution. The oral telling of tales also allows the teller to check the affective responses of the audience. When retelling such stories, the orderliness of the plot provides a structure upon which children can feel secure, whilst adding evaluative aspects such as vivid description, modern settings and dialogue or unexpected twists in the resolution.

Once a story has been told and learned and loved, it is part of storytelling tradition to adapt it, update it, unpick it and sew it back together in a different pattern. Some of this refashioning must work unconsciously. Bartlett's classic (1932) study is still influential in pointing to the way in which our recollection and retelling of stories is influenced by our affective response and level of interest. Whilst we tend to retain the broad structure of tales, the details of characterisation, description and ordered incident are forgotten or transformed according to our temperament and our personal, evaluative reaction to the original.

When children attempt to tell their story to an audience, teachers will naturally be cautious about the danger of setting too great a challenge. Anyone who has seen young children struggle to read out their poem or story to the school assembly will realise that many children find it difficult to perform to large groups. But stories that allow for a well rehearsed narrator and repeated interjections from a chorus can be successfully managed. For most performances, however, the small scale fireside model of storytelling is more appropriate. Children can watch their audience and gauge the responsiveness of their listeners. Older children particularly enjoy providing special performances to younger classes.

Once children have learned and performed stories, teachers can use this ability to support their narrative writing. I have found traditional tales to be the single most popular and successful means of stimulating children to want to write stories. The first time I told the Italian tale, *The Land Where One Need Never Die* to a year 5 class, their hands were little blurs as they rushed to retell the tale in writing. In line with Bartlett's study, the resulting stories showed that children recollected different features of the tale and changed or emphasised particular aspects whilst keeping the key structural elements.

How can the child writer help the reader to imagine the story they are writing? Traditional tales are often light on description, but some key images can be fixed in the reader's mind. It is useful to support children's attempts at descriptive writing by asking them to draw on their own ability to visualise. They can visualise both real and imagined landscapes and walk around in them.

I used this technique when children rewrote *The Fisherman and the Mermaid*, and kept prompting them to use *imagined* sensation. A mermaid's singing can be imagined and the crashing of waves against rocks can be heard in the imagination. The feel can be conjured of loose, hot, kickable sand, or firm sand that blanches slightly underfoot. Children can imagine walks across different forms of sand: ribbed and hard as stucco; sand with warm pools inhabited by tiny one veined fish; sand piled up over their legs on a holiday beach; the sand that gets into sandwiches; the sand that shines like a silver tray when they turn to look towards the sun. Much of this visualisation and imagined sensation and hearing happen automatically when we read or hear stories, but young writers need to be guided to make use of them to render their written stories more real for their readers.

As folktale collectors once fumigated and spruced up earthy folktales to produce fairy tale entertainments for aristocratic audiences, so it is open to you as a teacher to collect tales and rework them for today's children. Kevin Crossley Holland experimented with reinventing old tales in his *British Folk Tales* (1987), in which he refashioned several stories in modern settings. As part of our Traditional Tales module we ask students to adapt tales and to justify the changes they make in terms of their critique of the original story and their own purposes.

Critical evaluation of classic tales leading to informed adaptation and retelling has become increasingly common in primary and secondary schools. This has partly been influenced by the lead given by authors who have rediscovered, adapted and reinvigorated traditional tales, such as Angela Carter, Roald Dahl, Raymond Briggs, Alan Ahlberg and Tony Ross. Equally influential are the writings of scholars and educationists such as Marina Warner, Jack Zipes and Harold Rosen.

Exploring traditional tales

Myths and folktales lend themselves to a variety of useful language based activities in the primary classroom. Programmes can be planned to examine and critically evaluate specific stories and to devise creative responses through what are called directed activities relating to texts (DARTs) and through *spring-board* work in which learning is broadened to include analysis of wider social contexts.

Teachers will be able to devise their own programmes of study under these two headings, but the potential for work in this area might become clear when we look at teaching strategies that we have used.

Some approaches build on children's shared knowledge of classic fairy tales, using their familiarity with plots to support work at sentence and word level. One activity that is popular with students on teaching practice is storyboarding. First the whole class and the teacher decide on a set number of key moments in a specific story. In groups, the children then create a series of tableaux, showing the main scenes from the tale. These can be photographed and attached to a wall mounted display to show a comic strip portrayal of the story. Depending on the attainment goals of the teacher, speech and thought bubbles devised by groups of children can be added to the comic strip. A narrative block underneath each picture can provide a coherent, continuous narrative. When revisiting this technique the teacher can expect each group to take greater responsibility for producing the complete text. Further extension of this work can lead to children's transformation of thought and speech bubbles into dialogue on a page. Narrative blocks can become paragraphs.

After a gradual withdrawal of collaboration and scaffolding, children can write a complete version of their favourite tale on their own. Such genre-switching activity helps children to achieve greater control over writing for different purposes. It should always follow an initially enjoyable engagement with the classic tale.

The skill in choosing DARTs activities is to match the activity to the text. *The Jolly Postman* books by Alan and Janet Ahlberg are good models – Humpty Dumpty, for instance, appears as a jig-saw to be put together again. DARTs work can help children to explore writing in a range of genres: Goldilocks can write a letter of apology, a wanted poster can be devised for the big bad wolf.

In Key Stage 2 teachers can explore the issue of gender stereotyping of characters. Depictions of strong female characters in collections such as Carter's *Virago Book of Fairy Tales* (1990) can stimulate discussions about the character traits of the heroes and heroines in traditional tales. In some cases this can lead to retellings in which the attributes of the traditional hero and heroine are redrawn. A girl in one of my classes rewrote *Cinderella* as the tale of an older sister who always had to do more chores than her younger, prettier siblings. When I asked her about this she explained that she had younger, blonde twin sisters and she felt that she had to do most of the chores at home whilst they got most of the love and attention.

Thematic approaches will often include both DARTs and springboard techniques. The legend of the *Pied Piper of Hamelin* can be explored through folk-tale versions and Browning's narrative poem. Historical examinations could include work on the plague and the Children's Crusade. Recent official guidance has led to a resurgence of such thematic programmes of learning in which the knowledge and skills of specific disciplines are retained whilst children are helped to make connections between their learning in different subject areas.

From the personal to the traditional

In order to focus on traditional tales I have left my real starting place till near the end of this chapter. Perhaps the best place to initiate storytelling is with the lives of the children in your class and the tales they've heard from older members of their community. Before discussing children's personal narratives, I will consider what we know about the underlying structures and language features of shared narratives.

Labov's studies (1972) of the storytelling skills of black adolescent males have had a lasting influence. He was particularly concerned with analysing grammatical complexity and storytelling style. The narrator's evaluative comments – the descriptions and emphases and the stance taken by the narrator – were as crucial to the success of the story as the account of events.

It is possible to extend the style and structuring of children's personal stories – especially stories for performance. In his 1986 study of Texan oral narratives, Richard Bauman described some of the recurring structural features of tales told amongst a group of working class, male adults. His analysis of comic tales showed that stories told about personal experience tend to be organised from the beginning in light of how they will end. The narrator has learned to control the amount of information he reveals. When reporting on their own experiences and those of others, the tellers organise their material in a recognisable pattern: moral characteristics of the main protagonists are established, along with indicators of time and place. The narrative builds towards a pay-off line. If you think of some of the stories that you retell, you may see that they follow this pattern. This delayed disclosure is a feature of fictional narratives. Skilled raconteurs also adopt it when telling factually based or apocryphal tales.

I find that some children can already use delayed disclosure in their personal anecdotes even before they leave primary school. Their techniques are partly honed by their audiences. When we tell stories about ourselves and others we adapt our tales to the reactions of the listeners. We grab their attention, we build up our tale and we try for a significant climactic ending through gradual revelation and evaluative comments and descriptions. In this book we have tried to collect some examples of the sharing of personal histories with children – often told by people in the local community.

But personal stories are also a natural starting point for children's own storytelling in class. This can then be selectively extended into written accounts. The preference for personal narratives in the writing of children has been established in studies over the last forty years (see for example, Wilkinson 1971, Rosen and Rosen 1973, Burgess 1973) and appears to arise from their everyday speech. It is easier for children to adopt and develop these skills in oral news and storytelling activities.

When they move from personal and contemporaneous stories to retellings of traditional tales, teachers need to model the special language and generic features of traditional storytelling. Carol Fox (1993) and others have discovered the ways in which children can capture the distinctive language features and structures of literary genres in their playful narratives from a young age. Her study focused on the recorded tales of five year olds whose parents had read them a range of literary fiction from the first year of their lives. The same understanding of distinctive genres can be found when listening in to the commentaries of boys as they play football; and accompany the game with a sound track that mimics the commentaries they have heard on TV. Children asked to make up and 'perform' an advertisement adopt the terminology and accent (often American) of professional advertisers. Children in role-play often use the characteristic speech and demeanour of their teachers.

Children are not as familiar with the multiple genres of traditional tales and oral storytelling as with recent genres. As a teacher you may have to think carefully about storytelling as an event, as a formalised happening with its defined cues for the children to adopt in their role of listener, responder or teller. When working with young children, you sit in a 'storytelling chair' and wear a storytelling cloak adapted from a dressing gown or degree gown.

Props can support the telling of tales; for instance, listening to the sighing of the mermaid in *The Fisherman and the Mermaid* with a large shell clasped to your ear. However, the main purpose of props is to ease the transition from this world into the world of the story: a special world, but one which will exist in children's minds. There are many things working in your favour as a teacher. You know your class and the type of story that will engage them. Unlike the professional storyteller, you do not need to learn numerous stories for every occasion. You can find four or five you really like and then make them your own.

Once your story is underway, your own visualisation will support your telling. Stories proceed through a series of concrete events. Folktales eschew sub-plots and detailed description is limited to a few special items. Stories for children often invite joining in and repeating memorable lines. The telling is scaffolded for you by the patterning of the tale. Most of all, if you have chosen well, you will be supported in your telling by the faces of the children, as they sit mesmerised by the ancient magic of your tale.

Teaching traditional tales to support writing
Christine Seton

> Here Chris Seton explains an approach to teaching traditional tales to mixed age classes in a semi-rural school. She shows how children can learn in an enjoyable way to adopt the language and techniques of storytellers and how the ability to perform an oral retelling can support writing in a range of narrative genres.

Scout Road Primary in Mytholmroyd is a small school of 105 pupils. We have a Reception class and three mixed age classes. Three years ago our Assistant Headteacher went on a course about the importance of oral storytelling in helping children to establish a narrative style, making it easier for them to improve their story writing.

We have since decided that traditional tales will be taught once or twice a term to each class. The Reception class concentrate on the fairy stories that were already the basis for some literacy teaching: *Goldilocks, The three little pigs* and *The Three Billy Goats Gruff.* Teaching for older children involves consideration of more complex tales, including Hans Anderson stories, stories from diverse cultures and biblical stories such as *Noah and the ark* and stories from various faiths.

The arrival of the *Primary Framework for Literacy and Maths* (2006) and our earlier adoption of topic-based work suggested by *Excellence and Enjoyment* (2003) entailed some alteration to our list of chosen stories in both Key Stages. For example, the *Quest* strand in literacy in the *Framework* led us to adopt The *Firebird* as a story to focus on in years 3 and 4. The *Fables, myths and legends* strand prompted us to choose a Robin Hood story for years 5 and 6. It was interesting to see how well our new emphasis on oral retelling fitted in with the revised literacy strategy, as it helped to justify the work we were already doing.

The teaching

To help children to learn new stories, we devised a sequence of activities to support recall and performance. The initial teaching takes place over three days. On the first day the teacher performs her version of the tale and – after some discussion – repeats it. In Key Stage 1 and sometimes in the mixed Year 3 and 4 class the children act out the second telling of the story in mime.

On day two the children join in with parts of the tales and use expressive actions. Then they draw a story map to help them remember the structure of the story. This is not only enjoyable; it also fixes the narrative structure firmly in the children's minds. So the visual learners have something to hang onto, since up until now this has been solely an oral and kinaesthetic exercise.

On the third day the children tell the story to a partner before possibly performing part of it for the whole class. During this phase retelling can be attempted in small chunks, with feedback after each stage.

What happens next depends on what our aims are for each particular group of children at that time. In Reception there are play activities. In Year 1 and 2 the children generally write the story. In Year 3 and 4 they might turn it into a playscript or write an alternative ending. For *The Firebird* they devised in pairs a more elaborate and humorous version of the story than the one we had provided. They focused on the contrast between Ivan's stupidity and the intelligence of the wolf and then they retold it orally.

In the mixed Year 5 and 6 class they sometimes write a modern version of a traditional tale.

Whatever is done, the quality tends to be high. Not only do the children not have to devise an original story, they also have the narrative voice in their heads – a voice that able children have from their own reading but that they all have after learning their own version of a traditional tale. The less assured children enjoy the confidence that comes from knowing what they are writing about and the more confident enjoy adapting and improving a strong basic narrative.

In Year 3 and 4 the children were split into groups and divided the tale of *The Little Mermaid* between them. Each group rewrote the tale as part of a play script. Each group's script was put together and photocopied so that every child had a copy and then they performed the play. It was a challenging task for 7 to 9 year-olds, but the resulting written work was extremely good. Because the tale was fresh in their minds, they could concentrate on aspects of drama such as the layout of the script and use of stage directions – their targets – rather than thinking what to write next. The slightly old-fashioned tone of the original narrative was a model for their own writing and this was a valuable outcome of the exercise.

Conclusion

The National Literacy Strategy makes it clear that children need to read texts before they can attempt to write in that style or genre and the *Revised Framework* acknowledges that listening to and re-telling a story enhances children's narrative writing. Teachers know that it is the children who read stories who find it easier to adopt an appropriate narrative tone in their writing. Teaching a class to tell a remembered story gives all the children the appropriate authorial voice for their own writing and gradually improves their writing style. For example, the emphasis on connectives in context gradually familiarises children with them so there is no need to resort to tedious worksheets. Working with traditional tales is an inclusive activity, it is fun to do and it enables pupils to access challenging writing tasks. It's definitely worth a try.

The Patchwork Quilt

Wendy Holland

Wendy Holland reflects on more than 30 years of storytelling practice in a variety of settings and the challenge of sharing stories with deaf children. She starts by looking back to her own childhood and finishes by discussing storytelling with today's young children – especially her own grandchildren.

Stories were woven into my childhood, like the patchwork quilt my Aunt Dorothy had sewn from strips of soldier's khaki, squares of satin from a ball gown, rectangles of winceyette from tired sheets and ribbons of lace from the hem of worn out petticoats. Each piece had its own smell, texture and story. It covered the brass framed bed I slept in occasionally, with its lumpy striped mattress and stiff bolster pillows.

There were few books in the house: *The Ladies of Cranford* by Elizabeth Gaskell, a prize awarded for my once athletic aunt's part in a three-legged race on sports day. A leather-bound bible held at communion, placed on a dresser surrounded by willow pattern plates; and for some unknown and never explained reason, Alexandre Dumas's *The Count of Monte Christo*. The local newspaper was read avidly for its information about births, deaths and marriages or tragedies at sea.

We came from generations of seafarers. My great great great grandfather had owned fishing smacks that sailed from Great Grimsby, and this tie with the sea had remained through the generations. Hence the anxiety over news stories about ships sinking under the weight of black ice in the North Sea. In my aunt's generation, the men of the family were skippers or deckhands, and to perhaps stretch a point, fish merchants or dockers. During the war these reserved occupations had caused a schism in the family, with the young men who'd been press-ganged into service at the front declaring it unfair that others, because of their seafaring connections, got away 'scot-free' or so my Aunt Dorothy told me.

The house was crammed full of what in storytelling terms are 'artefacts', and in the days before I could read, they opened vistas on the world I have not seen to this day; pictures made from 'the sand of the pyramids': a carved ebony stick, brought back from the Boer War by my grandfather, along with its owner, a young black South African; a beautifully decorated tea caddy, from Ceylon; photograph albums full of uniformed young men with sombre or relaxed and smiling faces, or wearing swimming trunks and up to their thighs in some foreign sea, posing for wives and sweethearts. There were greetings cards with pieces cut out of them ('censored' my aunt said); post-cards – one I can still recall of a large troop ship that looked as though it was beached in the desert, until my aunt explained it was in 'Suee's Canal'. I knew canals held water, but who 'Suee' was I had no idea.

On balmy summer evenings, after I'd been sent to bed, I'd perch on the window seat with my older cousins listening to the men playing their mando-lins in an impromptu concert in the street, hearing the stories about Uncle Billy and his 'nerves', and why Tom only had a stump for his right leg.

My first five years were filled with stories. Some were part of my family's his-tory that was held in trust by my aunt, who took this duty seriously. Others came from my older cousins, who enjoyed filling my head with terrible fables just before lights out. I couldn't read when I went to infant school, but I could tell stories and, as an only child, I soon came to realise that storytelling gained you friends. I perfected my craft in junior school, aided by being able to read, which I did voraciously. I began a nice line in helping others finish their 'com-positions', until my class teacher, Mrs. Nickerson, detected an uncanny resemblance in the style and tenor of the endings, and I was sent to the head-mistress's office in disgrace, at a time when corporal punishment still held sway. It wasn't so much my stinging palms that curbed my addiction to story-telling that year, as the arrival of a television in the house.

It would be too simple to lay the blame for the loss of an oral storytelling culture on the advent of television. The decline, as Eileen Colwell (1991) and other commentators have pointed out, had begun years before, when news-papers and books took over from the storyteller's memory. Children still en-joyed telling stories. Now they mixed the heroes of fable with super heroes from the TV screen, acting out their fantasies in the playground as Captain Kirk or Batman slew the dragon/alien. As a young NQT in my first appointment in an infant and junior school in the middle of a large council estate near Leeds, I watched over and, when necessary, policed such dramas at play-time.

As a new reception class teacher with 44 children (and the assistance of a nursery nurse twice a week for baking and PE) I was fortunate to be guided by an inspirational Head of Infants. Anna was a natural storyteller and believed passionately that children had a right to be told stories and to re-tell stories themselves, particularly her charges, many of whom had never attended play group or nursery provision and whose lives were often marred by the conflict and poverty that surrounded them. Tall and usually quietly spoken, it was all the more effective when she used her 'commanding' voice to stop a child in their tracks. I've seen her hold the attention of 200 infants in school assem-blies, telling stories about the loss of something 'precious', or anticipating the arrival of someone 'special', re-telling and adapting myths and fables for her young audience. An accomplished pianist, she would use music to emphasise the drama of the story being told.

In her own classroom I would see Anna hot-seating a story, although she didn't know the term. She would drape a chair with bright material, don a witch's hat or Easter bonnet, to tell a story. She encouraged children to take their turn to wear the hat, sit in the chair and regale their audience. What Egan (1988) calls the cultural universality of storytelling was affirmed by the way these young children made sense of the world.

After several years in mainstream schooling, I moved to a local school for the deaf, determined to bring the wonder of stories to the children in my care. The nursery of the school took children aged 2 to 7 years, whose hearing ranged from partial to profound deafness. I had a lot to learn, not only about the condition but also about the school's 'aural' approach. This meant en-couraging children to use what residual hearing they had, rather than sign. The rationale was that if children used sign before they could speak, they would not develop the skill of using their voices.

How do you tell stories to young deaf children? I found that it was similar to the methods used with preliterate children who could hear. When one sense is diminished, you use all the others. So the adults used body language, ex-pression, artefacts, visual imagery and music to tell stories and the children did likewise when they retold the stories.

Food was a regular theme. The children tasted the 'gingerbread man' biscuits, the assortment of foods the 'hungry caterpillar' chomped its way through, sweets from the witch's house in *Hansel and Gretel*, and so on. Low frequency music vibrated through their bodies to emphasise the rhythm of the story, as they watched lips move and took in the 'variation of pace, eye-contact, gestures, mannerisms, physical jerks, quirks, twitches, fleeting grins, frowns, gleans and glares' (Rosen, 1988, p70). Children with partial hearing might also detect the cadence of the human voice.

When the children re-told their stories, traditional tales often ended differently. Peter, a four year old with partial hearing, was adamant that the fox would not eat the gingerbread man. Each time his group performed the re-telling, he would glide the gingerbread man off the fox's nose and, at the crucial moment, move it over to the safety of the riverbank. What ensued looked something like a rugby scrum, as the fox, the old man and the old woman jumped on Peter while he held the cardboard cut-out gingerbread man aloft until adults intervened.

In the days before digital cameras we took Polaroid photographs of the children telling stories, and used them in individual or small group work, to remind them about what they had done. In one session I introduced the book of *The Very Hungry Caterpillar* to Sophie, a profoundly deaf four year old. Sophie shook her head violently, stabbed at the book, then pulled it from my hand and threw it on the floor. Searching the room, she found the story box we had been using, pulling out the card and tissue paper butterfly that had been our story prop. I suddenly realised the reason for her anxiety: the picture in the book bore little resemblance to our homemade artefact.

It was clear that the children made links between personal experience and story. Once after a Summer Fayre at the school, Mary, a very active four year old, lost one of a pair of expensive post aural hearing aids (the kind that hook over the ear). The aid was never discovered even after metal detectors were brought in, much to the curiosity of the children. A few weeks later, I was telling a story about a toy going through the motions of looking and searching, when Peter suddenly tugged at Mary, pointing to her right ear, still minus its hearing aid, miming 'searching'. He couldn't articulate the words 'lost' and 'searching' but his meaning was clear.

Even though the children could not hear the storytellers distinctly, they still felt 'the rhythm of the binary conflict, the events that carry it forward and its resolution' (Egan, 1988, p24), establishing meaning in a confusing world.

Some years later, (after completing a Masters Degree in English followed by a spell lecturing to young adults), I returned to the classroom and young children. The staff and children at the nursery I joined were all great storytellers. Stories were told everywhere: sat on a blanket outdoors, hiding among the branches of the willow arches, in a hollowed out boat donated by a parent, in the sensory garden with its camomile lawn, on the bridge under which the troll lived, and indoors too. The rooms, as they changed their focus to reflect new seasons and themes were the impetus for many stories: a dark tunnel began the journey to The Dark, Dark House; a boat filled with animals echoed *Mr. Gumpy's Outing*, and *Noah's Ark*; a huge cardboard box took children to the moon, like the bear in *Whatever Next*.

One morning, a group of children listening to the story of *We're Going on a Bear Hunt* in the sensory room were using the room's special effects to make the grass swish, the snow storm rage and the leaves of the dark wood crunch underfoot as they searched for the Bear. When the story ended, one child pointed out that the Bear's shoulders were slumped and he looked sad. What if he had only wanted to play and was not about to eat us? The child was doing what children do when listening to a story: 'making sense of the world affectively as well as cognitively' (Egan, 1988, p29).

The question set children searching for well known and loved stories which had redemptive endings. Could the troll in *The Three Billy Goats Gruff* be forgiven? Several children who felt sorry for the troll resolved that he would be rescued from the water and given food on the condition that he let everyone over the bridge. Others thought he should survive but be banished.

At circle time argument raged about the 'baddies' in stories. What if they'd been misunderstood? The giant in *Jack and the Beanstalk* had been burgled. As for wolves, the list was long. Should Peter have trapped the wolf for the hunters? Could the three little pigs have befriended the big bad wolf? Perhaps if Red Riding Hood had shared some of the goodies in her basket with the wolf, he'd have been too full to eat her grandmother? If the bad fairy in *Sleeping Beauty* had received her invitation to the celebration, things might have turned out differently.

What impressed me about these discussions was their intensity. Children willingly took turns to hot-seat their particular view, putting on the story cloak or hat, trying to win over their audience as they recounted their version of the story. They became what Ted Hughes (1977, cited in Egan, 1988, p85) described as 'little factories of understanding. New revelations of meaning'.

Piaget (1951) talks of this pre-operational during the ages from 2 to 7 as the time children engage in animism – a belief in the ability of inanimate things to take on human characteristics. He highlights the importance of the intuition children use at this stage, which is lost or changed as they mature. I have a picture of my granddaughter, aged two and a half, sat on one of those rides favoured by supermarkets, staring at a life-size plastic model of Bob the Builder. She is leaning away from him, half fascinated, half afraid he will speak to her.

The explosion of language that occurs during these years, growing from a vocabulary of a few hundred words to thousands, can be harnessed creatively through the telling of stories. At this time in a child's development, the curriculum will hopefully be play based. As Vygotsky observed '...in play a child wishes and realises his wishes by letting the basic categories of reality pass through his experience, which is precisely why in play a day can take half-an-hour and a hundred miles are covered in five steps' (cited in Toye and Prendiville, 2000, p9)

The children's everyday experiences in the nursery often triggered stories. An experiment at the water tray, when the water had been coloured red resulted in a story about 'The Wine Factory'. I had been observing Liza, a four year old, whose sense of wellbeing was low, because she was missing father who was working in France. She and Paul, also aged four, were playing together, sharing different sized bottles and filling them, when Liza announced that her bottle had 'wine' in it, like the wine her father brought home from France. Peter said his half-full bottle was 'beer'. They pretended to 'drink' the wine or beer. Other children gathered round and Peter, the young entrepreneur, started charging his customers £1 a bottle for best beer. Not to be outdone, Liza charged £2 for *her* wine. After lunch that day, when the children who attended full-time gathered on the carpet to read or tell stories, Liza told this story (I have omitted her pauses and the interruptions from the audience):

> Once upon a time there was a little girl who lived with her mummy and big sister and her daddy and her dog, Jack and they were very poor, so her daddy went away to find some ... a job. The little girl's mummy worked too, but her big sister looked after her, but sometimes her big sister played with her own big friends and the little girl was left alone. The little girl went to the room daddy went to when he came home and ... it was a dark, dark room with spiders and ... and Jack barked. On the table was a bottle ... with wine ... it said 'drink me', so she did. The little girl started to fly ... up ... up and she flew to her daddy. The end.'

Apart from Liza's obvious sense of loss, there are elements of other stories she had heard; *The Wizard of Oz, Alice in Wonderland, The Dark, Dark House*, all fused into this original tale, evidence of her love of stories and the need to use storytelling to help her through a difficult time. This, as Margot Sunderland observes, is more helpful and supportive than 'reductionist literal statements such as, 'I'm cross' or 'I'm bored'. Feeling words can hide, whereas story can reveal' (2000, p35). Being able to find 'images and metaphors to express thoughts or feelings' brings relief and a renewed sense of wellbeing. Liza, at four and a half, was due to leave the nursery at the end of the summer term, but even some of the youngest children used storytelling in this therapeutic way. Susie, a three year old newcomer to the nursery, was coming to terms with having a baby brother. One afternoon she began to paint and this story emerged as she painted:

> That's a green stalk for a flower...that's a little monster and that's a bigger monster ... but it's got no teeth – the little monster ... see ... they're all friends. This is another flower ... stalk, this at the bottom [leaf] and this the top [another leaf]. A very, very big flower. These ... petals ... one ... four ... five. This is a circle (draws circle round the 'little monster'). It's a boinging trampoline and the little monster is boinging up ... up ... there [the top of the flower] and he finds a little house and the big monster chops, chops it the flower down. The little monster is crying now ... cos ... it wants its mummy ... but its mummy has ... has so many children she doesn't know what to do...

There are clear echoes of Susie's favourite story, *Jack and the Beanstalk* and a nursery rhyme, *The old woman who lived in a shoe*, as well as revealing some of her confused feelings about her new baby brother.

The storytelling sessions sometimes involved puppets, which 'liberate children's voices, allowing them to explore different speech styles and registers, intonations and language tunes' (Teresa Grainger, 1997, p124). The ability of children of this age to invest human characteristics in inanimate objects was apparent in the 'conversations' between puppet and audience and indeed puppet and puppet master.

It is several years since I worked in schools. As a link tutor, I glimpse snippets of brilliant practice around storytelling, but it is still, sadly, an underused and undervalued vehicle for making the curriculum accessible to young children and enriching their lives. Wells (1987) and Fox (1993), among others, provide clear evidence of the benefits of storytelling with preliterate children who 'display a degree of knowledge about narrative convention and form and linguistic styles and plot which is usually associated with more mature and highly literate readers and writers'(cited in Grainger, 1997, p35). Grainger also cites Paley (1981), who emphasises the benefits to reluctant readers of listening to complex oral stories that would be beyond their reach in printed form.

When I asked my grandson, George 'what do you want to be?' when he was twelve, he answered unequivocally: 'a writer'. But this has recently changed. Now he's an avid cartoonist; he spends hours moving the figures he has created, capturing them frame by frame, to tell the stories in his head. Making up stories has been something he has enjoyed since he was three years old. Even when he began to read independently, his bedtime preference was always, 'tell us' (he and his younger sister, Alice) 'a story, Nana'. I 'interviewed' him and Alice recently to find out what stories they recalled from infancy.

> **George**: *Mr. Bump*, because it was my nickname – I was so clumsy. Grimm's fairy stories and Hans Christian Anderson – *The Tinder box* – those dogs – they used to frighten me. Comic Book heroes, *Batman* and *Spiderman* and the bad guys you always got better background stories about the villains. Greek myths and English folktales, King Arthur, *George and the Dragon*. Creation stories, I like those. Roald Dahl, he's great – he always puts a twist in, like *The Emperor's New Clothes* and *The BFG*. I liked it too, when we made up stories, you know, when I'd begin with an idea, then Alice would follow and then you.

> **Alice**: (aged ten, accomplished singer and actor): 'You telling us stories. I remember one you told about a girl trying to grow a flower. I like listening to story tapes too – *Alice in Wonderland's* a favourite. You can use your imagination to picture the characters. That's why it's disappointing when you see the film, and it doesn't look anything like how you've imagined it. *The Tiger who came to Tea* – I loved that – I was mad about tigers at the time. So many stories! I prefer stories told in the first person, it feels more real somehow.'

Storytelling, sadly, seems to disappear in primary school.

> **George**: We wrote stories in Year 4 then read them out to the class, but that's not really the same as telling a story, is it?

> **Alice**: We do plays and we get chance to add bits ourselves, so I suppose that's like storytelling in a way.

Alice's response to film resonates with Betty Rosen: 'Even with very young children ... pictures in the imagination of the receiver of a told story have more impact than pictures in a story book' (1988, p19).

Rosen's observation is a fitting end to this chapter:

> ...to close the books, look at the kids, tell them a story from scratch, then ask them to tell that story back again...it puts the whole process into a new dimension. It presupposes an enormous confidence in people to know that something new and good will come from every child. (Rosen, 1988, p8)

For children's sake, we should all make that particular leap of faith.

A place for story

Sally Greenwood

Sally Greenwood argues that narrative based on oral storytelling and the study of traditional tales should still have a central place in the primary school language and literature curriculum. She draws from the approaches suggested by genre theory to argue for a structured programme to support the understanding of the features of myths to enable children to retell and write their own stories in that genre.

Genre theory

Traditionally, the teaching of reading and writing in the primary school has been associated with fiction and particularly story writing (Riley and Reedy, 2000). Halliday's research in the 1970s revealed that children experienced a limited range of genre in the primary classroom because teachers concentrated on fiction. This caused them difficulty when they encountered unfamiliar text types later in their school career. Influential publications such as Wray and Lewis (1997) suggested strategies for providing a more varied literacy programme in primary schools.

Following on from Halliday and Martin (1993) it was suggested that non-fiction genres are more significant in children's lives than fictional genres. These *significant* genres are primarily non-fiction texts and include: recount; report; procedure; explanations; discussion; persuasion. Genre theorists argue that if children are to be empowered they need to be able to read and write these kinds of text. However, as Riley and Reedy (2000) remind us, narrative is also significant in children's development. Narrative is seen as being central to the way in which children interpret events and express their reactions to experiences (Bunting, 2000).

Since children are immersed in narrative from babyhood it is through story that they can begin to understand their own lives. Although some genres may be considered more powerful in enabling children to take an active role in society, the role of narrative should not be underestimated.

Genre theorists assert that the purpose of a text will affect its structure, vocabulary and sentence organisation and that to develop into successful language users, children need to be made aware of the implicit rules associated with different genres (Stamboltzis and Pumfrey, 2000). The explicit teaching of the linguistic features of text has provoked debate. It is argued that knowledge about language is innate and it is through usage that children develop and extend this knowledge. Riley and Reedy (2000) use the example of children discovering rules for themselves, such as adding 'ed' to verbs to indicate the past tense. They argue that formal explicit teaching of linguistics is unnecessary and could even be counterproductive (p20).

Although it is beneficial to experience a wide variety of genres and be made aware of their linguistic characteristics, children must also develop an understanding of the contexts in which these are used (Bunting, 2000). Furthermore, as noted by Barrs (1994), genre theory does not always take into account children's development as writers. She maintains that children's writing is often a mixture of genres and does not reflect the adult genres identified by theorists. It is therefore essential that children's writing is seen as transitional. When it does not adhere completely to the adult structures, it should not be considered incorrect. Rather, it should be viewed as a critical part of the developmental process that children undergo as they gain deeper understanding of the more recognisable adult genres (Barrs, 1994; Bunting, 2000).

Pedagogical justification of a genre-based approach

The approach I advocate is modelled on the *First Steps* programme developed by the Education Department of Western Australia (1996) and subsequent support strategies developed by Wray and Lewis (1997). Although these models concentrate on non-fiction texts, children also benefit from this type of scaffolding when writing fiction (Lewis, 1999). Lewis talks about a 'five step approach' to developing children's narrative writing and the model she provides is closely related to genre theory and the need to teach the structural and linguistic features of different genres explicitly. One powerful genre I have explored with year 5 children is myth.

A myth is a narrative that attempts to explain nature. It is concerned with gods and goddesses and 'assigns human beings their place within the entire order of creation' (Crossley Holland, 2000, p15). Myths deal with death, sorrow and atrocities. Bettelheim argues that they are inappropriate for young children (1976) and that young children should be protected from the pessimistic and tragic nature of myths and that fairy stories are more appropriate. Bearne argues, on the other hand, that myths appeal to children because myths relate to the adult world, dealing with issues of love and death, good and evil. She maintains that children can cope with these issues at a remove, through story (Bearne, 2000 p187). Bearne advocates the use of myths with children, stating that children experience forces of love, hate and temptation and that myth can help them to explore these feelings. She believes that children have to realise at some point that 'things don't necessarily end happy ever after' (Bearne, p197).

The National Literacy Strategy proposed using myths with children from year 3 and it is probable that many teachers now include myths in their planning for Key Stage 2 English. These approaches can be exemplified in my own practice.

To begin with, children are immersed in the chosen genre. I provide several examples of written myths, carefully chosen to illustrate typical story structures and linguistic features associated with this genre. Children are given the opportunity to listen to me reading these texts and to read myths themselves. Carter (2001) and Grainger (1997) stress the importance of children listening to an experienced reader and following the text. Carter asserts that listening to another reader will develop a child's 'inner voice', thereby improving their comprehension when they read silently and when compose their own writing.

I also share myths with children through storytelling. Myths were originally conveyed orally without any form of reading or writing, so relating them is a particularly appropriate way of sharing this genre with children. The structure and style of children's writing improve if children are exposed to both oral storytelling and the sharing of written texts.

The genre based approach focuses upon deconstructing texts, as a precursor to constructing other texts using the same structural and linguistic features. If the texts shared with the children are typical of the genre, children can identify the structural, lexical and linguistic features. They need to be given a checklist of vocabulary and linguistic features and a story map representing the story structure.

The outcome of discussion on the structure of myths can be represented in the form of a story map. This effective pictorial method of representing narrative structure is particularly useful in stories where there is movement of characters from one setting to another. So it is appropriate to use story maps with myths (Riley and Reedy, 2000, p73). Once they have deconstructed the myths and represented the structure in the form of a map, children map out a familiar myth in readiness to retell it to the class.

Grainger (1997) highlights the advantages associated with storytelling by children. Storytelling enables children to develop their power of language through their choice of vocabulary, structure and style. It gives them the chance to display their creativity and knowledge in a way they might not achieve through writing, and it can also help children to develop intonation. Grainger argues that children will also use linguistic features they would not use in their writing. Once they have embedded such language in their oral repertoire they will find it much easier to use it in their written work. The oral process of storytelling should be seen as part of the writing process and no child should be asked to write a story until the story exists 'inside his (sic) head' (Grainger, 1997).

At this stage children can begin to plan their own myth. Some children are confident enough to move straight to the planning stage using a story map whereas others benefit from the use of a planning frame. Riley and Reedy advocate the use of such frameworks, which they see as 'a powerful way of focusing attention on the elements needed when composing a story' (p80). Their usefulness will be further enhanced through teacher modelling. I have found that some pupils benefit also from using picture prompts. Visual images are a rich source of stimulation when planning stories and using them together with a story map and planning frame can prove highly effective (Grainger, 1997, p52). Having completed a framework plan children are in a position to begin the final stage approach suggested by Lewis and Wray (1997): the drafting stage.

Conclusion

Children obviously lack experience of a variety of texts, the language associated with them and their structure. They require support and explicit teaching to distinguish the specific linguistic features, vocabulary and structure of each genre. Genre theory and the strategies that have developed to support teachers in the teaching of genre have proved useful. However, it is essential that children's creativity is not stifled and a balance is required between the formulaic genre based approach and a more process based approach where children are viewed as authors and where they are free to be creative.

Part 2
Storytelling across the curriculum

Tracking how tales travel
Maggie Power

After annual tests of the summer term ended Maggie contributed to work in a school which would be valuable throughout the following year. Children were moved into mixed age and ability groups to learn about countries of the world and she brought in a dimension on folklore.

Low Ash school

Low Ash is a large primary school with around 400 children in Wrose, an area that was once a village above Bradford and Shipley but has become a suburb linked to the urban conurbation. A few children in the group I worked with were of Asian British origin but most were from white middle-income families.

They were investigating the culture, art, geography and many other aspects of the different countries they studied. Much was left to the initiative of the teachers. In their mixed age groups, the children were introduced to a range of activities and tried out Indian dance, Aboriginal art and much else.

The aims

I wanted to share stories with one of the groups while making them aware of links between places. I wanted them to understand the reasons that we have a world heritage of tales: because of the movement of people now and in the past and because as people have moved they carried their stories with them. Sometimes these tales are in written form but for the most part they are in the heads of the travellers. I wanted the children to go home with a story in their heads.

First we discussed who told them stories. Their replies were similar to those from the inner city school I had worked in. The presence and influence of grandparents in the lives of these children was enormous. They were told stories by parents but especially by grandparents and even great grand-parents. We talked of journeys and movement; we talked of travel and ex-change before the times of aeroplanes, of messages passed on before we had telephones, texting or the internet. This is for children of today a world long past. We talked about people who travelled to different parts of the world and why they had done so.

We then moved on to consider the collecting of stories, the explorers who moved within and between countries collecting tales. One child volunteered to stand on a table at one side of the room and represent Africa, particularly West Africa. With a little guidance, he told us stories that the people in the area knew: the tales of a naughty spider, Anansi. Another child stood on a table on the other side of the room and – with support – told us that she was on an island called Jamaica in the Caribbean and she found out that the people there told their children stories about the very same spider. I asked the children why and how this might have happened. After some discussion certain suggestions were ruled out:

- there was no chance that mobile phones could have been used
- no, teachers had not given out printed versions in each country
- no, there was no email in those days so sadly no one could Google Anansi

We came to the conclusion that the stories had travelled in the heads of the people who had moved between these places. We looked briefly at forced movement, at how people lost their freedom but that it was impossible to take away what was in their heads. The children explained that they too could keep information in their heads and walk around with it still inside.

Then I told the story of how the spider tricked the tiger and had all the stories changed from being Tiger stories to being Anansi stories. The potential for development was immense. Had it been a single group of older children, year 5 or 6 perhaps, much more could have been done in the realm of travel and settlement. And younger children could be encouraged to find out in their history lessons whether invaders and other travellers brought their stories to their new land.

Reflections and implications

So many of our city schools serve children and families who have moved from one part of the world to another, if not recently then in the time of their grandparents or great grandparents. Schools able to incorporate and value their stories fulfil the requirements of the national curriculum but they also validate and affirm the children. To direct children to listen and record stories of movement in their own families is also to encourage them as researchers.

The history of even our most familiar stories, those that form the cannon of popular culture, can be sourced to areas of the world outside northern Europe. Yet when we deny them these links we miss an opportunity not just to widen children's understanding but also to empower them.

This mixed age group compiled a quick list of tales we were all familiar with and located them in areas other than a Disney film or comic or a book of fairy tales.

I informed them that a version of *Cinderella* exists in most countries, that it is thought that its source is China 'The earliest recognisable Cinderella story known to us is the story of Yeh-hsien, dating from the ninth century AD' (Philip,1989).

Philip identifies the earliest European version of the story as published in the 1630s, but the version which had the greatest influence is written in French by Charles Perrault, published in 1697.

I explained that *Aladdin and his magic lamp* existed in written form for many years before being staged at the local theatre and is part of the collection of the 1001 tales told by Shahrazad.

Red Riding Hood was another tale they all knew, but they did not know that it was recorded in central Europe centuries ago. Jack Zipes (1993) relates the history of the tale and examines its significance in *The Trials and Tribulations of Little Red Riding Hood*.

As a foundation for creative work, it is good for young children:

- to be introduced to the history of stories
- to know that stories have been changed and often exist in many different versions
- to know that there are many stories where the girls and not just the boys are brave
- to be aware that each area of the world has stories of worth just waiting to be discovered.

Talent, like narrative, is not exclusive to the few but is all around us waiting to be released. Talent does not hover above at a distance but is within us. The magic that will shift it into the open is the magic of stories, from the everyday experience of our own lives and from the corporate witness to the lives of those who occupied past cultures, which is the folk story. (Rosen, 1991)

And that is how I conclude this chapter, with the wish that the talent in our classrooms, in both the children and the teachers, can be stirred into life for the benefit of all. Stories offer schools an opportunity to release and nurture talent, to enhance the creativity of both teachers and children. We all have a need to work in an imaginative way.

I could see that the children were enjoying all that they were doing in school while I was there. The fun permeated the week. The teachers gained satisfaction from being able to follow their own initiatives, and took pleasure in working collaboratively across year groups and even key stages. The children were leaving classrooms talking animatedly about what they had just been involved in. The school – like many others – had grasped the opportunity to work out of the box. The time they allocate for this is usually towards the end of the summer term, in the post SATS window. In that period a place should always be reserved for narrative and the people who can share stories. We need to allocate time to celebrate those who travelled but took their stories with them.

Talking roots: the gift of oral history

Monica Best

After graduating from Bradford College Monica got a job working in a large infant school in Huddersfield. She is currently Year 1 team leader and has specialist responsibility for literacy.

As I reminisce on my life as a child in the 1970s, I realise that in some ways I led the kind of bohemian existence children these days can only regard with disbelief and wonder. I had an unconventional up-bringing completely alien to those growing up in today's safety conscious, sheltered and thoroughly risk assessed lives. At no more than seven or eight years old I scaled dangerously high coal chutes, swung across treacherous rivers and streams dangling precariously from tenuous lengths of threadbare rope, and encountered more than one odd and devious character cooling off in shady, damp and dense woodland during the height of summer. As the old adage goes, none of this did me any harm. These were the concrete experiences through which I learned about life.

My background as the youngest of four wayward girls spawned to a single Austrian immigrant mother made me what I am today – for better or worse. As children of a divorceé, the stigma at that time hung like a lead weight round our necks, and never more heavily than during my time in school.

I was one of two children in my class who didn't have a dad, so that made me hugely different. What made me even more different was that my mother was a foreign agoraphobic who kept me away from school more often than she sent me, simply because I was the baby of the family and Mum got lonely at home on her own. I didn't much enjoy going to school anyway, because the children mocked my broken English, littered with a local dialect courtesy of a broad and fiercely Yorkshire grandmother.

In consequence the rather strange Anglo-Germanic hybrid that I am stayed at home and, at my mother's insistence, immersed myself in the glorious solitude of mountains of books. Not that my mother was an avid reader herself: rather, she was an avid researcher. Reference books were her thing. Blessed with a head in the clouds but with feet firmly on the ground, her hobby was to enter competitions in hope of winning the fortune that would someday lift this lone parent family out of a poverty we didn't acknowledge at the time. She never did win the big prize, but as a parent she provided me with the richest form of cultural capital imaginable: a divine worship of all shapes and forms of the written word.

Note, however, that I refer to the written word. Spoken words were an entirely different matter. Ineloquent and awkward to this day, I still find it far easier to write than to articulate my thoughts verbally.

Although my mother urged me to read and study at every opportunity, I cannot recall a single time, any time, that she actually sat down and read me a story. I remember my older siblings teaching me to read (at the age of four I was already a fluent reader), but there were no bedtime stories, no nursery rhymes, no songs. As a busy single mother of four girls she simply had no time.

Thirty four years later and, ironically considering my dread of school, I am part of arguably the most rewarding and worthwhile profession there is. I am an infant school teacher. And perhaps the most ironic fact of all is that the children I now teach are just like I was way back then.

For the past six years I have worked in one of the largest and most diverse infant schools in Kirklees, a borough encompassing the once industrial mill valleys of Huddersfield. Our school, adjacent to a large and thriving council estate, is hugely multicultural, with an ethnic minority roll of over 70 per cent. Most of our children are of third generation South East Asian descent, although recent years have seen a significant rise in Kurdish, African, Polish and Polish Roma migrants. Most notably, our large sprawling catchment area is deprived.

Our children have colour, intensity, vibrancy and a real lust for living. They are willing to embrace anything and everything life has to offer. Their vitality and passion is reflected in their enthusiasm to learn. They know that their school is a place for learning, an environment that could quite possibly change the course of their lives. On paper our results may be below the national average, but what we give to these children in terms of *value added* means more than any figures in any league tables.

In recent years, teaching literacy through the National Literacy Strategy and more currently the *Revised Framework for literacy*, I have witnessed first hand the struggle some children have with what is still essentially a white middle class curriculum so far removed from their own concrete cultural experiences that little of it makes sense to them. The one area of literacy that highlights this most of all is that of traditional tales. *'Today we're going to write a story,'* I hear myself say. But can a story be written before at least a part of it has been lived, experienced, told and passed along? And in the telling and passing, does the story not become richer, embroidered with the colours of imagination and language?

As teachers we know that learning begins with first hand experiences. So how can we ask children to produce a brilliant piece of narrative without first ensuring it is something they know about?

In an attempt to equip them with the tools of the trade, we provide something concrete to set them on their way. Out come the puppets/ cuddly toys/ magic wands/ tactile objects/ stimulating photographs/fairytale illustrations etc. so as to fire their collective imaginations before we send them away to write something interesting for their audience. And if there should be so much as a spark of imagination, a flash of brilliance, a glimmer of inspiration from their six and seven year old minds what, as consummate and dedicated professionals, do we then go and do? We remind them of capital letters and full stops, finger spaces, correct letter formation, spelling ... and for heaven's sake just try and write along the lines!

When they think they just might be able to cope with all that, there are *Super Wow* words to remember, interesting adjectives, extended sentences, temporal connectives, an exciting plot, a good beginning, middle and fantastic ending (define the meaning of 'fantastic'), appropriate setting, interesting characters – good, bad, ugly, other ... And for the higher ability children and (heaven forbid) the Gifted and Talented, there are paragraphs to think about, inflections, subordinate clauses, verb clauses, irregular verbs, appropriate tense, prepositions, punctuation, metaphors, synonyms, and syntax ... does any of this make sense?

It occurs to me that what I've just written is a sad refection of current literacy teaching. Are we so concerned with teaching the technicalities of narrative and dissecting every text we read that we fail to take into account the enjoyment, spontaneity and reality of good stories? Do we ever teach our children that good stories come out of our heads and sometimes don't even have a beginning, middle or a happy ending?

By some chance, our school forged links with Bradford College as part of our ongoing CPD programme, years after my formal teacher training. I heard about the research Maggie Power and George Murphy were doing that focused on oral storytelling and knew they would be keen to work with real children in real schools. An oral storytelling day was arranged for the whole school and delivered by Maggie in three sessions, accordingly tailored for each age group.

Out of professional curiosity, and as a consequence of the children's obvious enjoyment of the oral storytelling sessions, I began to formulate some micro-research of my own. I set my Year 2 children the challenge of telling the story they had heard that day to someone at home, giving clear instructions that the story then had to be passed on to someone else by whatever means possible. We discussed the possibility of writing the story down and sending it via letter or email to relatives at home or living elsewhere in England or even relaying the story down the telephone. '*Is that OK?*' the children asked '*Don't we even have to be there?*'

The idea of the children having to be physically present to tell the story struck a chord. In some way, and rightly so, they saw themselves as key participants in the storytelling process, as having ownership of the whole process. Communicating a story via letter, email, phone or text was like parting with some precious pearl of wisdom or priceless jewel and not being entirely sure it would reach its destination safely. They regarded storytelling as something that had to be done face to face. Writing it down, sending it away or even '*giving it to the telephone*', as one child put it, simply wasn't good enough.

The story was duly retold but I gleaned little from the feedback. The children had forgotten parts, couldn't remember the ending and were anxious because it wasn't written down for them to read it 'properly' to their audience. In effect, what they were saying was they were frightened of getting it wrong. Has our teaching become so inflexible that we are failing to instil in children the confidence they need to articulate a story without the support of a text?

I began to wonder if stories were being told at home at all. The next challenge was for the children to ask someone, anyone, in the family to tell them a story. This way the teller would have physical presence and in the children's eyes what they told would therefore qualify as a real story. Their task was to feed back to the rest of the class three pieces of information: who told them the story, information about the characters and setting etc, and what the story was about.

This time the response was huge. We scribed a list of classics such as *The Hungry Caterpillar, Can't You Sleep Little Bear? Funnybones, A Quiet Night In, Handa's Surprise* and so on. The general consensus among the children was that these were '*good, real stories*'. The children were familiar with them and as they were part of the classroom library stock, they were borrowed time and time again to be shared at bedtime with parents and enjoyed by all. Clearly our whole school initiative to encourage reading at home with parents was working well. The children knew the technicalities of character, setting and so forth, and all was well and good.

But the fact remained that the stories children were sharing and being 'told' at home all came from books. What about oral storytelling? Is there a place for it in today's humdrum society? Is it happening at home? This prompted a beleaguered discussion in class: '*My mum tells stories wrong*,' Adeel insisted. '*She needs a book and pictures. She can't remember* The Gingerbread Man *or* Jack and the Beanstalk. *She gets the end all wrong*.' That there is a right or wrong ending for a story evoked vigorous nods and murmurs of agreement. It was a general cause for concern among the children.

'*My dad can't read so we say the pictures*.' Here was indeed a way in. It transpired that Chloe regularly adopted the role of teacher and she and her dad made up stories based on her knowledge of reading scheme characters and familiar stories and illustrations. It seemed that many families enjoy sharing books as part of the bedtime routine and this is something which the school is naturally keen to promote. But that was not enough. '*Does anyone ever tell you stories that don't come from books, stories that come out of their heads?*' I heard myself ask. Collective doom and gloom ensued and I was met by a sea of blank faces.

It seemed that many parents were busy working or caring for what were in some cases large extended families in Huddersfield and 'at home' in the tight knit communities with origins in South East Asia or, increasingly, Eastern Europe and Africa. I asked the children to indicate who had regular contact with extended families and, more specifically, grandparents. Most children indicated that if they were not living with or in close proximity to grandparents or if they did not see their grandparents at least weekly, they still had at least some form of fairly regular contact with them. So it appears that, despite current trends and media thought, grandparents play a significant role in the children's lives. I asked whether grandparents told stories and the answer was an animated and reassuring '*Yes!*'

When I asked about the type of stories told there was a distinct split. White British children mainly agreed that their grandparents read stories from books, which concurred with our earlier findings. The majority said that their nanas and granddads were '*not so busy*' and '*read long, long stories*'.

However, in our conversations over the following weeks a distinct commonality emerged. A significant oral cultural capital appeared increasingly among the children of every migrant background. In some cases parents and grandparents were illiterate and spoke little or no English. But that wasn't important. The key to real oral storytelling lay within these extended families. Moreover, it seems that grandparents are often central to sustaining the oral storytelling tradition. The single most important factor emerging from several of our discussions was the rich history of oral storytelling that permeates almost every ethnic minority background: an almost inherent urge to pass on through each generation the cultural capital of different types of stories; of mother country, religion, ancestry and family history. And interestingly it is the grandparents who are striving to keep their own histories and the histories of their children alive still by handing them, like family heirlooms, down through the generations.

Working with children has led me to analyse more and more of my own childhood and its influence on the person I am today. Like a thunderbolt the oral storytelling history I had stumbled upon resonated in my own personal experience. I had gone through life more than a little disgruntled because my mother had failed to read me bedtime stories. I felt I had somehow missed out on the many rich experiences other children were getting. Such an injustice!

But then I remembered how my mother could talk. While she was busy preparing the evening meal, while she was cleaning every nook and cranny in our huge Victorian home in preparation for Christmas Eve celebrations, the stories poured out. Each aged, fragile glass bauble she unwrapped from browning tissue paper came complete with its own story. Stories were told in bed late at night in the frosty room more than a few of us shared. And this was when it happened.

Stories of 'home', of Russian soldiers marching through the streets of Austria at the end of the War, of my mother's days as a dancer at the local opera house, of meeting my father, a sergeant stationed in Graz after the war. She told proud stories of a greatgrandfather who fought on horseback for the German army in the First World War, of an old aunt who ran the local pharmacy with her father, their own emporium of lotions and potions, coloured glass and brass scales. Of a Hungarian great aunt who was a talented concert pianist, of my mother's dedication to my grandmother as she battled against cancer. The tales went on. As for their accuracy, who knows? For despite everything, I now know my mother to be a storyteller supreme, ensuring that her history will live on through her daughters and their children. Would this be true for the children of migrants today? I dared to ask the questions and the answers came flooding back.

Aneesa's grandmother's story of her years spent as a girl in the mountains of Kashmir. Hamza's uncle who to this day sells rugs in the same market in Islamabad as his grandfather many years ago and who once made a rug for a prince! Anila's great grandmother who, curiously, was nipped on her toe by a tiger and lived to tell the tale! How Maimoonah's grandmother still finds England so chilly and has not yet found a way of keeping herself entirely warm and dry so wears long socks and 'PE leggings' under her shalwar kameez. '*It never rains at home*', grandmother frequently laments. Tale upon tale poured forth. It occurred to me that this is the starting point: a source of writing so vibrant and real that is personalised to each child. Real characters in 'real' stories told by real people whom the children can relate to.

My one regret is that this all transpired at the very end of a busy school year, at a time when the children were due to move on to the local junior school. Had time allowed, I could have pursued my research much further. And I could have used the children's own personal histories as the most effective scaffolds possible for story writing, using their own stories as a stimulus for writing. And what a stunning collection of tales we would have had to read, tell and pass on. What is so encouraging is that oral storytelling is still richly embedded in some children's lives. But, sadly, it remains a largely untapped resource in creative story writing.

If we were to question whether the theory of *Talking Roots* can be applied anywhere outside my own experience and my own classroom, the answer is: I simply don't know. I only know from observing the shining eyes and vivacious faces looking back at me as they tell their amazing tales that spoken family history matters. It matters to the children and their extended families. If this is not the basis for a traditional story of all stories for the children I work with, then I don't know what is. If these stories exist in other classrooms, the teachers need to capture and use them for the benefit of all.

A Tale to Tell

Dave Jones

David Jones is Headteacher of Holybrook Primary School in Bradford, who makes a difference by who he is and how he works. Here he offers an account of what inspires him and how he inspires others through narrative. In Summer 2008 he was nominated for a national award for his work. He won the regional final and everyone in his school and community shared in the success.

I n 2002 I had a book of school assemblies published. *Uncommon Lives* is a collection of forty biographies of people whose lives should inspire the young. Whilst it would hardly constitute a threat to the Rowlings and Morpurgos in the best seller lists it represented a high point in my literary ambitions. I was delighted to dedicate the book to my wife and kids as well as to my late sister. But I reserved pride of place thus – 'In memory of my late mother and father, who told me stories about life. For I consider their stories to be the most important influence to shape my professional life'.

About five years ago I attended a conference in Bradford at which the keynote speaker was Professor Charles Des Forges of Exeter University, along with others working in schools. The Professor's brief was to unpick the relationship between parental involvement and pupil performance. He stunned his audience with his opening remarks: 'I hate coming to Bradford!' Our attention was well and truly grabbed. He went on to explain his antipathy to the city: As a young man he was a keen supporter of Hull Kingston Rovers Rugby League Club and memories of defeats by Bradford Northern were the cause of his ire.

De Forges presented a critique of research relating to the theme of his talk from J.W.B. Douglas' seminal book of 1958, *The Home and the School*, to the present. That the home is an important influence on future achievement was taken as read. The Professor was interested in the *mechanism* by which parenting affects children's prospects. From his review of the evidence presented in the literature, he concluded: children are more likely to succeed when they come from a home where there is constant dialogue between the children and adults. As my dear old mum with her propensity for malapropism might have said, 'It's not rocket surgery!' Tell them stories. Talk *to* your kids; talk *with* your kids.

Professor Des Forges argued that the subject matter that underpins this nurturing conversational stream is of less import than the fact that it takes place. He said that around the hearth and dinner table of his childhood Humberside home, the main subject of debate was not ballet, classical literature or fine art. It was Rugby League and all things Hull KR. I was struck by the similarities with my own childhood.

I was the fifth of five children, born in the late fifties. My elder siblings were all girls so ours was a very feminine environment. My mother worked in textiles and my father was a coal miner, a Welshman who met my mum when they were serving in the forces in the Second World War. When hostilities ceased, they settled in Bradford and we kids began to appear at roughly two year intervals. In 1944 dad had suffered frostbite when his ship had been torpedoed and he had floated about as a lucky survivor in a liferaft in the Atlantic before being picked up and taken to hospital in Canada where he was told that the ordeal was likely to have left him 'barren'. I suspect that there were five of us because dad had a point to prove. The fact that I was the last of the line probably means I have the Canadian doctor to thank!

My sisters no doubt found little brother something of an encumbrance to their activities. I still only half joke with them that in my early years I thought my name was 'Dowehavetotakehim'. In the years of post-war austerity, where toys were at a premium, I suspect I was used as a substitute doll. My father returned home one evening from his subterranean toil to witness his only son dressed in girls' apparel, being pushed in a pram and for him – more worryingly it seemed – enjoying it all. In an age long before political correctness, he expressed concern that I was in grave danger of becoming a sissy or worse. So it was decided that I should be made a man of. Rugby League was to be my salvation. A red, amber and black scarf and pom-pom hat were knitted and thus garbed, I was dispatched to Odsal Stadium with my father. On 4 August 1964 I saw my first game and hitched up with Bradford Northern. It was love at first sight – the colour, the noise and the sheer drama of it all. I was smitten and, sadly, remain so to this day. Coincidently, that first game was against Hull Kingston Rovers and they won! Following the conference almost forty years later, I sent a copy of the front page of the programme to Professor de Forges for his office wall.

The relevance of this personal history is that as well as being saved from a life of sewing and flower arranging, I discovered my dad. Prior to the fateful day of my induction into the Rugby League fraternity, our contact had been merely domestic. Now we shared something other than mealtimes and annual holidays to Bridlington. From now on, from boyhood to late adolescence and beyond I had him captive and got to monopolise his attention for hours at a time. Home matches were great but better still were the trips on Wallace Arnold buses to away games across the newly created M62 corridor.

My dad left school aged 14. In the harsh economic climate of the thirties, educational opportunities were as narrow as the coal seams worked by lads who were not yet old enough to shave. For his generation educational opportunities were sparse and access to learning was gained through the lending library of the Workers' Educational Association. Despite a truncated formal education, my father was well read and a natural communicator. Possessed of the kind of bardic eloquence bestowed on so many of his countrymen, he loved to tell a tale. His heroes were champions of social justice – Aneurin Bevan, Kier Hardie, Paul Robeson and Annie Besant. On our weekly jaunts he regaled me with stories of their exploits. At the Boulevard after we'd watched Hull against the Northern, he showed me the photo in the clubhouse of Jack Harrison, the only professional player to be awarded a VC (posthumously) for his heroism in World War I. At Wigan he explained how Billy Boston challenged the racist gibes of ignorant fans to become a giant of the game. Dad's repertoire was endless and to me, never short of riveting. The seeds of my fascination for biography had been sewn.

At Hill Top Primary School I met and fell for an elderly spinster called Miss Davies. She was the Head and at unpredictable intervals she would arrive in our classroom with a book from her extensive Ladybird *Histories of the Great and the Good*. These visits must have been a way of giving our beleaguered teacher Miss Busfield a well-earned sanity break; long before the universal right to PPA time was won. These interludes provide my fondest memories of school life. I particularly recall the story of Nelson and his exploits wrestling polar bears and dying heroically. Florence Nightingale was another favourite and as Miss Davies turned the book to reveal the nurse's image to us, haloed by her lamp, I would gladly have kissed her shadow.

It is now clear to me that these twin influences at home and school were instrumental in shaping my career path into education. My route to primary Headship followed a circuitous path, taking in a spell as a youth worker in the East End of London and later as a History teacher at Secondary level. I eventually became Head in a 9-13 Middle School before being appointed Headteacher at Holybrook Primary in 2000 when Bradford LEA reorganised to a two tier system.

The newly created school is situated on the Ravenscliffe Estate. According to government statistics, the surrounding area is in the top (or should that be bottom?) 5 per cent of socially deprived communities in Britain. In the 1990s, Ravenscliffe and its environs became the recipients of a regeneration grant. Unfortunately, the final budget was denuded of several millions, which were taken to reinvest in the housing stock as a central feature of the regeneration programme, so there was little improvement locally.

Local people hoped that this interest in the plight of the area would generate improvements. Unfortunately, the estate has fallen into increasing dereliction and decay and the residents still await the long promised regeneration. Many houses are boarded up and some streets have been demolished leaving wasteland, which attracts vandalism and fly tipping. The severe deprivation which many of our families have to endure is not of their making and it is an indictment of a society which purports to be committed to the eradication of child poverty.

Holybrook was created following the closure of two schools on the estate, as part of the reorganisation of the city's schools. The area had become notorious for its low educational standards. The secondary school which served the community was the only one in Bradford to be closed in the reorganisation. The former middle school, in which Holybrook is now situated, returned the poorest KS2 SATs results in the city in the final year of its existence. This highlights the magnitude of the challenge the staff and governors faced in establishing the new school.

But not all was doom and gloom. We had two great things in our favour. One was that the only way was up. And there was no established culture, so no resistance to change. The opportunities for innovation and risk taking were embraced by a staff team that was firmly committed to the view that if you keep doing what you keep doing, then you keep getting what you keep getting. It was an exciting time and we were aware that we could do things rather differently.

Visitors to the school often comment on the impact of the biographical stories deliberately used throughout the school programme. It concerns me that the primary curriculum grows narrower as emphasis is increasingly placed on Literacy and Numeracy. As the Americans would have it, to argue against producing literate and numerate kids would be to decry mom and apple pie. That is not my intention. But we should not sacrifice breadth and balance on these twin altars of the curriculum. I fear that the humanities and creative arts may be squeezed out as we place greater emphasis on the SATs. Even Ofsted seems to tip the wink to an unbalanced educational diet as long as Literacy and Numeracy seem in order. As educational leaders it is our duty to light a candle rather than to curse this curricular gloom. If there is indeed a colonisation of the curriculum by these twin giants, then we must find other opportunities. We must fill up all the other nooks and crannies of the programme with stories to fuel the collective imagination of our students. Assemblies, displays, theme days, inter-school activities, visits and guest speakers can all contribute to this process.

Popular historian Simon Schama once said that history's role in education ought not to be to revere the dead, but rather to inspire the living. The claim that society is going to the dogs is not unique to the current era but perhaps there has been a moral decline in recent years. Whether or not this is so, the media have certainly created a perception that knife attacks, promiscuity, teenage pregnancies, drug and alcohol abuse and lack of respect for authority are symptoms of a malaise which threatens to hasten us to hell in a handcart. Education must be challenging if we are to grow the type of positive citizens who will be tasked with tackling moral turpitude in the future. There needs to be an epidemic of morality in our schools and this can be fired by studying remarkable lives through the ages.

Breaking history down to the experiences of individuals enables children to empathise with people from the past. Each year on World Peace Day (21 September) we remember Sadako Sasaki, a young Japanese girl who contracted leukaemia after the Hiroshima bomb. Sadako was entertained by her nurses during her long, monotonous and painful hours of treatment. They made paper cranes for her out of the paper labels from medicine bottles. According to legend, as she knew, to make a thousand paper cranes was to be granted a wish. Her wish would be for health. Sadly, she died when only 600 birds had been made, but Sadako's classmates continued her work and completed the thousand paper cranes. The story spread throughout Japan and beyond. People all over the world made cranes and sent them to the devastated city. A peace park and monument was built for these paper tributes to be hung and now there are millions. Each year our pupils make paper cranes and write their wishes for peace, and we mail them to Hiroshima. It is a practical way for children to feel empowered and realise that peace begins with them.

Remembrance Day has received greater attention in recent years and far more people observe the two minutes silence than in the past in memory of the fallen. It is an opportunity to honour those who die in wars. In Bradford, the council has instigated 'Pals Day' on 1 July each year to mark the anniversary of the terrible day in 1916 when the 31st Division of the Prince of Wales' Own West Yorkshire Regiment, the Bradford Pals, suffered devastating losses on the first day of the Battle of the Somme. We study the impact of this fateful day on the city and have adapted the words of a song written by Mike Harding dedicated to the Accrington Pals who were similarly decimated. Together with two local folk singers, the Hall Brothers, we recorded the song, and sales of the CD raised several hundred pounds in support of the Lord Mayor's Appeal. The Mayor invited the children to perform the song live at the commemorative event in City Square before being feted in City Hall with what they described as 'posh nosh'.

Our research for the project on the young soldiers led us to a website dedicated to footballers from the city. The children were amazed to learn that Donald Bell of Bradford Park Avenue was the only footballer to be awarded a VC in any war. But we also discovered that Bradford City lost nine players in the Great War, and the children gathered as much as they could of their personal histories. The school council wrote to the city planners suggesting that nine streets be named in their honour when our estate is rebuilt. The children were delighted to receive an official letter on council notepaper informing them that their idea had been accepted. I pointed out that when they are walking their grandchildren down Linton Way or Comrie Street, they can tell them that it was their gramps who had the street named in honour of these brave men. One will be named in honour of a footballer called Harry Potter.

I remember the impact that a widely told story had on me when I heard it for the first time when a young teacher. A college principal in the United States who was a survivor of a Holocaust death camp quoted it to his staff at the start of the academic year. It is old but not something to be lost in the troubled world of today.

> I am a survivor of a concentration camp. My eyes saw what no one should witness – gas chambers built by learned engineers, children poisoned by educated physicians, infants killed by trained nurses, women and babies shot and

burned by high school and college graduates. So I am suspicious of education. My request is that you help your students become human. Your efforts must never produce learned monsters, skilled psychopaths, educated Eichmanns. Reading, writing and arithmetic are only important if they serve to make our children more human.

Learning should never take place in a moral vacuum. At Holybrook we strive to use days of national commemoration – Holocaust Memorial Day, World Peace Day, Remembrance Day, Pals Day and Martin Luther King Day, to generate a moral debate and to raise awareness that as Edmund Burke the Irish philosopher is credited with saying; 'All that is needed for evil to flourish is that good people do nothing'. But how do we teach these difficult topics in a way which does not disturb our pupils? Can any of us, adults or children, fully grasp the true horror of the trenches, the magnitude of Hiroshima, the sheer scale of 6 million Jews erased from the map of Europe? Perhaps not. But we can offer some insights by using the testimony of *individuals* and we can inspire children with the message that even when evil prevails, people can achieve great heights of courage and selfless sacrifice to help others. Everyone who challenges injustice is like someone casting a pebble into a pool and sending forth what Bobby Kennedy termed 'ripples of hope'.

For the past five years, our pupils have been invited to Bradford's Cartwright Hall to participate in Holocaust Memorial Day. Each year we prepare for it by considering one individual's experience in this dark phase in history. Last year children learned about Corrie ten Boom, a gentile whose family hid Jews in Haarlem in Holland. They paid with their lives, sent to camps where all but Corrie perished. The children learned how she devoted her remaining years to counselling survivors and former Nazis. She believed that 'If people can be taught to hate, then they can be taught to love'.

After the ceremony of memorial, an elderly lady approached me and held out her hand. Her eyes twinkled and her tiny frame suggested a youthful, lithe grace which belied her eighty plus years. Still with her hand in mine, she told me 'I was a hidden child in Belgium'. Tears appeared in her smiling eyes as they did in mine, as I realised that this amazing human being was a surviving Anne Frank. She said that she was not alone. She, Bronia Veitch had recently attended a conference for hidden children in the United States along with six thousand others who are still alive to tell the tale. Bronia introduced me to Haneke Dye who had been hidden in Holland.

Some weeks later the two survivors came to Holybrook, bringing photo albums, forged papers and artefacts, including a small unopened tin of tea marked with the badge of the Scottish Co-op that Haneke had been given by a young soldier of a Scottish regiment who had helped to liberate Holland from Nazism. They held Year 5 and 6 spellbound with their testimonies. We learned how a man saved Bronia's life. He held Bronia's hand as he walked her away from a processing camp in preparation for transportation to God knows where and told her softly, 'Choose a new name'. We were told how Haneke and her friends cheated capture with the help of Dutch resistance workers. Fearing that an informer had revealed the whereabouts of her and her friends in a convent they posed as German Gestapo, 'recaptured' and rehid them before the real Gestapo arrived.

The two survivors spoke to groups in the morning, as scheduled. They stayed for lunch and, in response to the insistence of the children, they stayed and talked with us for the rest of the day. How uplifting it was to realise that in the face of darkest evil, ordinary folk will make the plight of another their own business, even under threat of death. The pupils surpassed themselves in the writing they produced after this memorable event. That is the power of story.

But Ofsted would say: this is all well and good but does it affect *standards*? Last year we received a letter from Lord Adonis at the DCFS to congratulate everyone involved with Holybrook on being the 23rd most improved school in Britain over the last four years. Whilst I regard league tables with the suspicion bordering on contempt, as do many of my colleagues, it at least means we get a truce from excessive scrutiny and an opportunity to focus on the real business of education. The first duty of the teacher is to inspire those in their charge. I hope that long after memories of 'sentence level work' or using 'morphology and etymology' to spell unfamiliar words have faded, these stories about life will resonate to inform the lives of those we have the privilege to teach.

Storytelling as a starting point for work in geography and history

Howard Lisle and Kate Cleary

Howard Lisle has for 38 years taught geography to children, beginning teachers on ITT courses and experienced teachers as CPD. To Howard, narrative has always been a powerful means of bringing alive geographical events, places and landscapes and their relationships with people. His intention is to develop a 'geographical empathy' that helps to explain the associated *geographyness*. Narrative can be used to enhance the delivery of primary geography and also, as Kate Clearly shows, history.

Teachers can tap the wealth of narrative material available and can extend normal classroom explanations of events or geographical concepts. Narrative can add a personal touch, assist the understanding of the cause and effect of events and the response of people who were there. The immediacy of news stories, for example, makes understanding a volcanic eruption and other events much easier for young geographers, and even better because we can see the people 'on location'.

Getting to grips with narrative

Reflecting upon my use of narrative in teaching geography I am convinced that many of the actions taken in 1970 provided an important and generic range of techniques that explain how to make more of accounts, narrations and stories of events and experiences. At the time there were few stories that could be successfully used to illustrate geographical concepts or events. Essentially there was 'too much story', as the authors clearly did not expect their works to be treated in such a geographically and analytical way. And unlike today, few were illustrated with wonderful pictures.

I found that articles in non-fiction magazines such as *Look and Learn* had sufficient material in a concise and condensed form to use as a springboard for lessons which build upon the narrative in the page-length articles. I could transport my classes to deserts and mountain summits, to the depth of the oceans and go on board aircraft, giant super-tankers and underground systems. There was a wealth of geography between the covers of the magazines at a time when it was the teacher who established the curriculum.

Visual material had to be still photographs or hired 35mm film in heavy metal canisters, so the empathetic narrative was important. *Blue Peter* and the summer expedition also provided material, but at this stage of my teaching there was not yet a VHS recorder to keep a record!

News reports were my staple supply of narrative and travellers' tales were equally useful. Explanations from mountaineers, for example, as they reached the summit and surveyed the view from the Top of the World, or the single-handed yachtsman trapped in a hurricane and mountainous seas that made him feel as if he was 'a nut beneath an elephant's foot'. Reading these accounts with dramatic effect opened the pupils' eyes to events and experiences they themselves would never have. News reports became my staple supply of narrative.

Why relate these approaches of years ago? Because today I am doing exactly the same, only with DVD, internet news reports, *live* footage of the hurricane and interactive whiteboards. This means pupils can now interact with events instead of being passive recipients of accounts of them. Past skills are producing the future use of such powerful narrative.

Displaying topical news events around a world map as a Window on the World Wall gives pupils an ongoing element of geography. The floods of 2007 and 2008 in England could be illustrated and explained through news reporting on TV and in newspapers and internet articles. This has to be better than studying a flood that took place many years ago and to incorporate the narrative of then with now.

A story to tell from times past

Kate Cleary looks at the importance of studying History in the primary school in working with and through the stories of people's lives.

History is about people and the study of their lives provides many opportunities to develop knowledge, understanding and skills in relation to the national curriculum for history. In this way the content and the skills and processes can be brought together. At all stages there can be opportunities to incorporate storytelling.

At Key Stage 1 pupils should find out about their own lives and those of adults around them, and also about the lives of significant men, women and children drawn from the history of Britain and the wider world. It is up to schools and teachers to make a selection and offers a way to make the primary curriculum more inclusive. It also provides schools with an opportunity to welcome in members of the local community and listen to the stories they have to tell. Children can be encouraged to collect stories from their families and friends. Sharing them in groups gives children valid opportunities to build their experience of telling stories.

At Key Stage 2 pupils should be taught about people and personalities in local, national and international history from the recent and more distant past. Although some of these individuals are specified in the curriculum, there is still the opportunity for schools to make their own selection too. An appropriate choice could help to meet the requirement to make links between the history of Britain and the rest of the world e.g. Akhbar, who was Emperor in India at the same time as Elizabeth I and who corresponded with her. With the teacher in the role of storyteller, there are opportunities to bring story sharing into the heart of the classroom.

To start with telling a story and then build on that introduction either in History or Geography is to:

- develop and enhance understanding
- open a door into a subject in a way that is both enjoyable and valid
- encourage children to collect retain and in time retell stories.

RE and story

Maggie Power

Here Maggie reflects on all that happens at the Cathedral described in the next section in the light of the current situation in relation to the teaching of RE in primary schools.

U sing national guidelines, each local authority produces a syllabus for religious education so that the work done in schools is planned locally. Faith schools have syllabi produced especially for their schools. All schools have to introduce children to Christianity but also to the major faith groups that are represented in schools and communities.

Religious Education The non-statutory framework was published in 2004. It has been of use nationally to support and guide members of local Standing Advisory Councils for Religious Education as they work to construct or amend their local documentation.

Teaching Religious Education in primary schools requires two key attainment targets: that children learn about a faith and that they take from this knowledge something to reflect on and consider in relation to their own lives.

The syllabus in Bradford is an exciting one. It encourages an approach that is creative and inclusive. What happens in schools is supported by visits to places of worship. The Cathedral in Bradford is at the centre of work giving children knowledge and understanding of one faith in this rich and diverse city.

Caroline and her team also affirm people of other faiths and none during visits. They show the peace chapel with a candle lit at all times and there for all to sit by as they hope and pray for peace in the world. They also point out the memorial to the Bradford football stadium fire where many of the Asian families from neighbouring terrace houses came out to try to save lives and give comfort. The children are also told of the doctors who, because of that fire, have developed an expertise that is used internationally to help victims of burns. All are stories to be told.

The work has many links to *The non-statutory framework*. At the Foundation Stage extensive reference is made to the place and value of story. In the section on personal, social and emotional development are examples related to experience and opportunities for religious education, for instance:

- Children use some stories from religious traditions as a stimulus to reflect on their own feelings and experiences and explore them in various ways
- Children reflect on the words and actions of characters in a story they are told and decide what they would have done in a similar situation. They learn about the story and its meanings through activity and play

At Key Stage 1 the section on learning about religion states that children should be taught to explore a range of religious stories and sacred writings and talk about their meaning. The section on themes also makes links to story and indicates where children should be introduced to the importance of certain stories and know how and why they are sacred and important to members of a particular faith.

At Key Stage 2 the importance of encountering religion through listening to visitors and paying visits to places of worship is listed under experiences and opportunities.

The section on learning about religion indicates that children should be taught to 'describe the key aspects of religions, especially the people, stories and traditions that influence the beliefs and values of others'.

The Cathedral is one of the many places of worship in Bradford that makes such work and opportunities possible. In 2007-2008 they had 2,500 booked visitors from Bradford but also from many schools in the north of England and beyond.

In most schools visitors come in to tell stories from a faith related to the history of a group, their values or celebrations. They provide an important stimulus to children's understanding and reflection. The story can be told in the classroom but, as Caroline Moore shows in her account of work at the cathedral, it's especially meaningful when children hear it on a visit to a place of worship.

The Power of Story – in Bradford Cathedral

Caroline Moore

Caroline Moore has worked at Bradford Cathedral for some years. The programme she has developed meets the needs of the various groups that visit. It starts from a respect for all. The use of story permeates all she does. She says she is introducing children to a giant story book of stone, one that is 13,000 years old and one where their visit can provide the next entry in that book.

A story begins

A coach threads its way through Bradford city centre, toils up a steep hill, and discharges its young passengers into the gardens of the Cathedral. Excitement and anticipation have been building steadily during the journey. The children make their way to the building, noticing inconsequential things – a gargoyle, a 'secret' staircase – but may not notice the big square Tudor tower looking down on them. Their imagination and curiosity are well and truly hooked. This wonderful place offers unlimited scope for their imagination. Inside, the space, the height, the arches fill their vision with colour and light, candles and angels. They are not overawed. Windows are at their level, to be explored later. It's a cathedral on a human scale. They are welcomed by the education team, who are the storytellers in a day full of story. The teachers sit down, relieved to have arrived, and sip the cup of tea or coffee that is quietly handed to them. While they relax and take in their surroundings the children's attention is engaged.

Bradford Cathedral is an ancient building full of surprising beauty, warmth of welcome, and a wealth of opportunities for discovery. It is a living building, home of a lively community, where history goes on being made. It has responded to change down the ages, reflecting the life of the city. As well as

Christian worship, it is a place of music and the arts, education and community, healing, hospitality and care. It has its feet on the ground and its head in heaven. It is very much a place of story, and a lot of its story is about its special sense of place. This site has overlooked the development of the city from a settlement beside the Broad Ford in Anglo-Saxon times, to a great industrial city, once the world's wool capital. Now it is a post-industrial multicultural city, a proposed City of Sanctuary for many nationalities. The history of the city is a quarry full of rich stories to unearth, and many of these are embedded in the fabric of the Cathedral, or linked with its community. Thus, in this place, we ensure that the past is not forgotten but is rather interpreted with care or celebration, turning story into occasion, informing the present and helping to create a future of hope.

Learning outside the classroom

Like cathedrals all over the UK, this building is a prime resource for learning outside the classroom, because of the scope it offers for bringing together fact and imagination. Every cathedral has a special 'wow' factor, and there are stories waiting to be interpreted afresh. 'Story' can be discovered, told, experienced, or expressed even without words. New stories keep happening, and become folded into the mix. With RE as the main focus, Bradford Cathedral can be explored across the curriculum, in tailor-made visits connecting with ongoing studies. The bulk of school visitors are young children but we also have some GCSE and A level students. Also, we welcome children who have special educational needs and who enjoy the tactile environment and relaxed atmosphere; pupils from referral units and specialist organisations; and overseas ESOL students with very little English.

The essence of a city

How do we make a big place with such complex purposes and uses come to life for children, some as young as five? It is my job, with a team of volunteers, to translate the essence of this wonderful building into meaningful experience and memorable images. Tell the stories of the folklore of a place enough times, and something special happens – something is hammered out which reveals the essence and character of a place or a time. Bradford's legend on its coat of arms is 'Progress, Industry, Humanity'. Countless stories are condensed into those three words, summing up hundreds of superhuman efforts of reform, invention, generosity and compassion, to overcome poverty and build a better future for its people, who were so dependent on the wool trade.

One such story is of William Scoresby FRS, master mariner, whaler, arctic explorer and renowned scientist. He came to this church in 1839 to be Vicar of Bradford. And he used his skills to establish and pay for eight schools for the poor in the city, and improve its living conditions. We don't just tell his story, 'Icebergs and Inkwells', we also explore the concept of creative thinking.

Story book in stone

In my welcome, I sometimes tell the youngest children that they have come to a giant story book in stone, 1300 years old. Every day turns a brand new page and today will bring a story that hasn't yet been written. It will be their story – and they will share it with their friends on the way home, tell it to their families this evening, and maybe still remember bits of it to tell their grand-children in years to come. They will hear many different stories, but of two main kinds – the Christian story, and the story of the place where we live. Both are ancient, but always new. Two thousand years of Christianity have provided riches to explore through story. The Cathedral is made of solid Yorkshire stone, and yet, in a sense, you can see straight through its walls. The stories let you see people who lived long ago or on the other side of the world. The stories of the building are written in stone and glass, in wood, and textile, in sign and symbol – like text messages on a mobile phone, waiting for someone to decode them.

Our programme

Visits are structured in a series of half hour sessions through which groups rotate. This has to be so well organised that they are hardly aware of the organisation – only of the content. Every group of children is made up of individuals unknown to us, with whom we need to build a meaningful experience in a bare half hour, seven times in a school day. This is where the power of story comes into its own. Our approach is to lead children from the familiar to the unfamiliar. The youngest children begin by engaging with the building, looking for things familiar to them – chairs, table, pictures, books, lights – and contrasting those they see at home with the ones at the Cathedral. And all the time, we are building the story of the community who belong here and worship here, why they come, what they do, who they worship – facts drip-fed as a basis for further stories, while also giving children their bearings and familiarising them with the place – the home of a living, changing community, of whose story they are part today.

Telling key Christian stories

The key tenets of Christianity, 'Love God, and Love your neighbour', underpin key stories, fundamental to exploring Christianity. The building is full of wonderful built-in visual aids, which can tell a story sequentially. A general tour would take in both history and Christian basics. A theme-tour can be made of windows which show the life of Jesus. Another tour called 'Roots' tells a wider Christian story chronologically. In doing so, however, we can assume nothing, – for instance, although most children know the story of the Christmas window and of Good Friday (another window) there are gaps in their knowledge. Children name the gifts of the Wise Men to the Christ Child as 'Gold, Frankenstein and Myrrh'. Some may ask why Jesus is shown as a European so we show other depictions by artists from many traditions. The question 'Do you know what happened two days after Good Friday?' evoked the reply 'Bank Holiday!'

We move on to look at the Easter window, then break to work on a short piece of drama, in which we explore the meaning of these stories. This medium enables children to express a spirituality they might not have the words to describe. Although children have heard, seen and experienced something of the Easter story, it is natural to talk about how the stories spread as people gossip about what they had seen, and how some followers of Christ found themselves in danger. Alongside the Easter window are four William Morris windows depicting the early martyrs, whose lives – and deaths – added fuel to the stories which swept the Roman world and eventually reached our shores. Windows showing Patrick, George, Andrew and David bring us to some well known stories from our own country. Older children may have time to look at evidence of people who lived out their faith in modern times.

Worship tour

The Worship Tour, which partners Roots, moves from font to Communion rail. It examines the places and tells the stories where the landmarks of life happen in the faith community – baptism, confirmation, marriage and funerals. On the way, it also deals with how and when people worship, by looking at holy books and prayer kneelers, and at the place of music in worship in the Chancel, and at what Holy Communion is about, in the Sanctuary. Again, misconceptions abound. A child just taught about the Font and Baptism asked 'If you haven't been baptised, can't you go any further into the church?' Another group listened to information that the name 'cathedral' means the place where there is a 'cathedra' where the bishop sits when he comes to his cathedral, ie the proper term for the bishop's throne, or seat of authority. To help them remember, they were told 'it is cathedral without an 'I'. A little later, one child, with eyes sparkling, asked 'when the bishop goes to an ordinary church, does he sit in a chur?'

Story walks

Story-walks take a group of the youngest children to a comfortable area, where they are told a story with religious significance which features an animal, such as the parable of the Lost Sheep. The children are then taken on their own special tour, their observation enhanced as they search for some more animals in windows and carvings. Each leads to a discovery – and a mini-story about the feature.

Local history

Likewise, stories from local history are told in different formats. Two particularly colourful stories relate to Bradford and its Cathedral. The first concerns the medieval symbol of the boar's head, which appears on Cathedral kneeling cushions. The hunt of a wild boar which showed up the true character of local huntsmen – all of them brave, though one was dishonest – and how the integrity of one of them won the day.

The other is about the Battle of the Steeple. This occurred when Royalist Troops in the English Civil War attacked the town and the stronghold of the church tower several times. The story was witnessed and written down by a local apprentice boy. In the final and decisive battle at sheep-shearing time, local defenders brought tools as weapons and were inspired to defend the tower with wool packs. Thus the ordinary became the stuff of legend. The tower was saved, but the town was ransacked. A bronze plaque commemorates the story, and the coat of arms depicts a wool pack alongside the crossed keys of St Peter. Children may come across this story in a tour, or in observational drawing, or presented as a dramatised story by a costumed actor.

Candlelit cell

Dramatised storytelling is also used in one of our key RE experiences. The Chapel of St Aidan can be blacked out, and lit with candles. The children are told that they are going on a time-journey, back to the origins of Christianity in the North of England. They are prepared for entering through the doors into semi-darkness. As they enter the candle-lit space, they find St Aidan or St Hild 'at worship,' singing ancient plainchant with Latin words. The saint will turn and greet the children and tell them some of their life stories, and of their monastic communities. Aidan will recite the Lord's Prayer in Anglo-Saxon, and end by telling the beautiful story of the healing of an injured village carpenter. Hild's graphically enacted story features the sparrow which inspired a Saxon king, and culminates in the story of Caedmon and the angel. The semi-darkness allows the listeners to become anonymous and be carried by the story. The chapel features a striking wooden cross carved with journeying figures, which is a good visual aid for 'life at the monastery'. There is no interaction in this story, no demands, just a chance to explore at many levels – historically and spiritually – the contrasts between life then and now. Children can reflect 'anonymously' on a story of self giving and dedication to God. Both enactments tell a moving story which creates an ambience as well as offering the possibility to introduce the eyewitness accounts recorded by Bede.

Dramatised Bible stories

Quite separate from this experience, we also teach sessions of mime or visual storytelling, which allow children to experience a role without having to worry about delivering words. Warm-up exercises, based on observation and memory, give a bank of recent experience from which to draw when we present a whole story in freeze frame of several pictures telling the story. Good storytelling is absolutely key to the experience, as it enables children to overcome their lack of confidence or self-consciousness, and to engage with the meaning and expression of the story.

Bible Stories which are brought to life include the healing of the blind or lame, the Good Samaritan, or Crucifixion and Resurrection. There is a progression from initially directing children 100 per cent to gradually incorporating their ideas. This economical format offers a discreet way of containing and directing energy with unknown children. Every group will produce something different to the same format, and can produce remarkably moving images. Adults watching them are frequently very moved. Three small cameos stand out. A tiny five year old girl in pink wellies, acting as Jesus, reaches up on tiptoe to heal a much taller 'blind' man. A small boy in callipers whose balance was unsure, compensates by moving his arms and hands with extraordinary grace to depict the same story. An intensely shy adult acting as Jesus with another acting the blind person, closed his eyes because of his self-consciousness, creating an image of Jesus 'entering the darkness' of blindness in solidarity with the blind man.

On the other hand, imagination sometimes catches you out. Children's mixture of worldly wisdom and new understanding can sometimes confound. A group of girls from a local grammar school preparatory department had just heard the story of the Good Samaritan, and were turning it into drama. Instead of pouring on old-fashioned olive oil onto the wounds of the robbed man, Good 'Sam' grabbed her imaginary mobile phone and rang the Yorkshire Air Ambulance!

Unspoken messages

Stories happen in many ways – visually, audibly, silently, through music, through mime, through experience. Stories draw on the senses, on experience and observation. The choice and structure of our programme has evolved over the years, keeping in step with national curriculum, the local agreed syllabus, and trends in teaching. But always the core questions are the same: What are our key stories? How can these best be taught and experienced? Who are the children? What angle do we need for these particular children? How can we best use the building for this experience? What is the overall balance between listening and doing?

This is a place that provokes reflection, and creative writing – not always on the day, but after the children have had time to take it all in and produce their stories, poems and letters. Sometimes these tell a powerful story in a few well chosen words of description. Sometimes their description is married to a flight of fancy – what happened to the missing angel? What is the secret of the blocked doorway? What is the legend of the steps to nowhere?

And what are the stories in this place that are without words – the silent messages of the building, and the stories of people connecting with it? Some of these are to be found in the book of Intercessions by the pilgrims' Chapel of the Holy Spirit, written by both children and adults. Or they may be evidenced only by the candles, which have been left burning on behalf of a group. Some are in the visitors' book, or the thank you letters and drawings. Others are glimpsed amongst the business of a school visit – a girl delighted to discover a ladybird in the Lady Chapel; a boy who discovered the date of the Battle of Waterloo on a memorial to be the same as his birthday; a Muslim girl delighting in a window depicting 'Maryam' wearing an embroidered head veil like her own; a small visually impaired girl who walked with difficulty, who found a patch of sunlight on the heated marble floor of the Chancel beside the bishop's throne, and lay there on her tummy 'swimming' in sunlight and crooning to herself.

Picture the profoundly deaf teenagers who stood in the choir stalls with their hands on the music desks, watching the organist play music they could not hear until the volume was such that they felt the vibration coming up from the floor and through the wooden stalls. The enormous smiles on their faces made an unforgettable picture – and reduced the organist to tears at their delight. There are so many other stories of the reactions and responses. A thirteen year old excluded from school stood before the WW1 memorial window with its graphic representation of a fallen soldier, and the crucified Christ. He gazed at it open mouthed, then asked 'Why did they do that to *him*?', pouring out his feelings about his own exclusion.

Behind almost everything we do in Cathedral education, there is likely to be a story. Stories keep happening and we have to keep observing and hearing, and re-telling them in fresh ways. Stories are part of the living fabric of the Cathedral, and they bind themselves into the experience of all who come to visit.

Working in Schools
Maggie Power

Where do I start? Stories are a wonderful gift to mankind. A good storyteller can leave an everlasting impact on a person. I still remember the stories I have listened to from my grandma. Even though she is not with me today her stories keep her alive in my heart. I keep the tradition of storytelling in my family and my children always prefer me to tell them a story rather than read them a story. (Seema Bhutto, Hindu faith tutor, Inter Faith Centre, Bradford)

In this chapter, Maggie describes her work in a Bradford primary school during the summer of 2008. This enabled her to reflect again on the importance of narrative but also to gain insights on what adults and children think of the importance of story. The focus is on RE and faith as a source of narrative.

The school

I spent time in Lilycroft school considering the importance of faith and story in the primary school. Lilycroft is situated just opposite Lister Mills and in the shadow of a large new police station, in the heart of an area of Bradford that is largely occupied by Asian British families of Pakistani origin in terraces of back-to-back houses where the workers from the mill once lived. The school has been here since the late 1800s and has seen its catchment change as the area has experienced waves of immigration. It is now a thriving school at the heart of the local community with a settled catchment, served by able and committed teachers. There are just over 400 children on roll. All the children are of ethnic minority background, most British Asian Muslims, though recently the school has welcomed a small number of children who have arrived from Eastern Europe. All come with English as an additional language but within that there is a wide range of exposure to and ability to work in English.

As with many schools in the area a good deal of the childcare is provided by grandparents, some of whom speak only Punjabi. The ability to operate across two languages is something that needs to be understood and valued in all schools. Children in many of our inner cities operate across and between cultures and languages and in doing so carry the stories of one into the other.

In their reading and book fortnight the school focused on incorporating text and story right across the school. After one of the teachers attended some in-service work in college, I was asked if I would like to tell stories to the children. I was keen to make the time and space to do so and provided a day of telling and sharing with children in key stage 2. I worked with two year 5 classes, two year 4 classes, for an hour each, then with two year 3 classes for half an hour each.

My intentions were twofold:

- I wanted to find out what their experiences were of listening to or being told stories at school and at home
- I wanted to share some stories with them, to give them stories to carry back into their communities

With each group I started with some questions –

Who tells you stories?

What languages are used?

When are you told stories?

Do you enjoy them?

Do you think teachers should be encouraged to tell you stories?

Who tells you stories?

The answers were numerous, varied and encompassed many from within family groups. Here are some of their written responses:

My mum tells me stories in Urdu and Punjabi, sometimes my grandma tells me stories. I like to listen because they give me ideas. Sometimes I think of pictures in my head. (Mehr – un nisa Raja Year 3)

My granddad tells me stories about his family and his ancestors. Sometimes he tells me stories that are funny, scary, sad but they are still stories that I like. (Maria, Year 3)

Do you enjoy being told stories?

Stories are good because they cool your brain and freshen your mind. Stories help you. (Kiran, Year 4)

It is good to tell stories because when you grow up you will be more confident because you have done it before. (Zahra, Year 4)

I think it's good to tell stories because when you are bored and upset people read you a story and you are happy. And I think you should also tell stories because when you read you can't stop. (Sumayyah, Year 4)

One group was hesitant at first. Some of the children thought that no one told them stories. They were read to but not told stories in school and they could think of no one who shared stories with them at home.

I started to tell them a faith story, one I know most Muslim children are familiar with. I said I knew a story that was important to children who were Muslim. I asked them if they had ever heard the story of the Prophet Mohammed *pbuh* and the woman who did not like him and swept her rubbish on to him as he walked past her house every morning. There followed a small eruption in the class: *Those* stories! Yes of course they knew those stories.

Such stories were told and shared within and across families, by grandmothers, fathers, mothers, brothers and others. The children became excited and suddenly enthusiastic about sharing information about faith stories. We were suddenly up and away! And I listened.

I wondered how often the opportunity is provided in school for children to share in the classroom what is offered to them at home. They told me that family members wanted them to know and understand the importance of many of the tales of commitment, stories that their families hoped might influence how their children would develop as young British Muslims growing up in West Yorkshire.

There are, I am sure, issues for many of our schools about how we work to incorporate stories from a faith, any faith, into the school curriculum. There is a need to create opportunities for valuing, considering and using stories from a range of faith backgrounds. In some cases these are the stories they know from home and so enable the link between school and family to be strengthened. It is important for children of all backgrounds to be introduced to stories that celebrate common values and standards and exist across all beliefs and none.

I told them a story I had heard over ten years ago in a family home in another part of the city, told in Punjabi by a grandmother. Her grandson was trusted with the task of translating it for me and others from school who were there listening. I was then working on a project for collecting stories from members of the community, which we recorded and put on a video and made available for use in educational programmes. The children did a lot of the work: they translated, they filmed and they helped with the editing of the film *Our Grannies*.

> There were two bulls that lived outside a village in Pakistan. One morning they realised that they had eaten all of the good grass and there was little left for them to eat. They set out on a journey; they travelled far until they came to a grassy area in a clearing just at the edge of the forest. They were happily enjoying the taste of the young sweet grass when they looked up to see that in front of them was a fierce lion, a lion who they were sure saw them as lunch.

> But they stood together and together they were too much for the lion who, after seeing how strong they looked as they stood as one, retreated into the forest as quickly as he had come.

> All was well and should have been for some time. The animals returned to their homes but then started arguing with each other. They each started to claim to be the stronger and the braver and to be the one who had saved the day.

> Unable to settle their argument they returned the next day. The lion was still there and they went forward one at a time, to prove their bravery. But as we know, the lion was now very hungry, as he had had nothing to eat for two days, and on their own each was weak and sadly each was defeated and killed by the lion.

The unspoken message from the grandmother was that each of us can accomplish only so much on our own, but that working together in school and with our families we can achieve much more.

The story was retold in an interactive manner. Children were involved in creating atmosphere with sound effects and some also took the part of the animals. These were supported in being given the words needed as we listened and shared. I would describe my feelings as a hungry bull and the child taking that part would repeat them to everyone else. In that way the child is involved but not vulnerable in having to find words for himself.

The children were asked to evaluate the story and then say who they could tell it to when they got home from school. They were enthusiastic and positive and I later heard that many of the children were able to carry the story in their heads and tell it to friends and family, old and young.

Reflections and implications

The work in Lilycroft Primary School will go on. Many schools are moving forward in their intentions and aspirations considering what they hope to provide for the children in terms of a creative and enriching environment in which they can grow and learn. For some time the view has prevailed that we can work from work sheets, we can drill and prepare the language work in school and expect our results to improve year on year. But as we come to reflect on the need to provide and to enrich we recognise the need to restore the role of the teacher as a giver and sharer of what is new with the children.

Children who are growing up within a faith community in Britain are very likely to know various stories drawn from the faith of their family. In some cases these are added to in places outside the home. Muslim children hear stories in the Madrasa and sometimes in faith assemblies in schools. Classes in Gudwaras introduce children to the stories of Guru Nanak and other re-nowned Sikhs. And stories are told in Sunday school for the children who attend while their parents are in church.

So there is a wealth of experience and knowledge that exists outside school. We need to build and strengthen the bridges across which we can draw from a wealth of material for all children to listen to. There are so many themes common to all faiths and cultures and if we could only identify links and tap into this wealth of material there would be a way to construct understanding and grow as one.

With every use of a story that comes from a faith tradition we need to say clearly which tradition uses it.

There needs to be an acknowledgement of the origin, along the lines of:

- We are going to listen to story about ...
- This story belongs to and is told by members of the ... faith
- It tells people about their history
- It relates to a special time when ...

All this links to work that covers the first attainment target in relation to teaching RE to children in primary schools. It relates to gaining information about a specific faith group. It enables children to know more about a specific faith tradition and this can all be done through narrative.

If we then ask children to examine what can be learnt from understanding the message that a certain story conveys, we will be developing the skills in relation to the second attainment target.

What can those who are not of that tradition learn from a story?

We need to ask:

- What do they learn from it or begin to think about?
- What can we as individuals in a class or school take from that story and apply to our own lives?

Some stories commonly used in the primary classroom link readily with those from a different faith. The three monotheistic faiths, Judaism, Christianity and Islam have a common bond that needs to be acknowledged – many of the stories are shared by all three traditions. I have taken work from a local school into college that shows how children have looked at the creation stories as found in the three different faiths. All are about Adam and Eve. Some content may differ to a degree but there is clear common ground. There are tales about Moses – *Musa* – Noah and the Ark and many more in each of these religions.

In Bradford, as in some other areas of England, schools with an intake that is not Christian in origin can apply to the local Standing Advisory Council for Religious Education to have a determination that allows them to have separate faith assemblies once a week. In our area we have the Inter Faith Centre, funded mainly by the local authority, in this case SERCO. They can provide schools with faith tutors who will lead assemblies. I have worked with the group of faith tutors to look at ways in which stories can be animated; children can be involved in both the telling and the dissemination.

Fatima Ayub, one of the faith tutors who works in schools and also with children in local Mosques uses stories to enhance and strengthen her work. She says:

> Telling stories from a Muslim perspective is important. When you tell stories to children you try to captivate their minds by forming mental images so they can grasp and understand concepts like good and bad, fear and hope, kindness as opposed to selfishness and the importance of love and mercy.

> The Qu'ran has many stories about the Prophets and lessons to be learnt from different nations. The life of the Prophet Mohammed (*pbuh*) is a story we tell the children so they can learn the moral messages from his life, for example, to be honest, to be responsible, to love all humans and animals and to take

care of the environment. Stories provide children with vivid illustrations of what happened so they can relate to it. They can take ownership of their stories and feel proud and this leads to valuing themselves and building their confidence and self esteem. Through stories, children think about and reflect upon their own lives and try to make it relevant to what they have learnt through challenging and stimulating the imaginative powers they think with. This enables them to develop their understanding and learning. Stories are a powerful medium to convey moral messages that impact on the lives of individuals.

Regarding religions

A book was published some time ago which took stories from each of the main traditions and looked for common themes. Each story was selected by members of the faith group and teachers were encouraged to use them in local schools. As it was a European project, the same stories were being shared in classrooms in Holland, Denmark, Ireland and two cities in England: Birmingham and Bradford. The book is no longer in print but the principle has been established and is, I believe, one we should return to. There are common themes.

All faiths and communities have stories that address key themes and values that are essential to all. You can find stories in each faith that illustrate the need to be honest and not tell lies, and consider them alongside each other but also alongside folk and traditional tales such as that told by the black slave Aesop about the boy who cried wolf just to relieve his boredom. It is fascinating how a story may be rooted in one culture yet versions have appeared in different communities that adapt and grow into another culture. The story told in Gujarati collected from a grandmother from India became 'Don't Cry Tiger', where the boy who was told to look after the goats now protects them not from a wolf but from a tiger.

To enable children to reflect on how many of our stories have common roots and to investigate and find similar themes in stories from different faith traditions is something we should aspire to do in primary classrooms. All of us working in schools also need to ask the children and listen to them so we can discover what is shared and valued at home.

Part 3
Performance

Passion and storytelling

Clare Muireann Murphy

In this chapter, an Irish storyteller explains her love for storytelling and discusses the approaches she has used in several community projects, including the Storytellers in Schools programme.

My love of stories harks from my earliest memories: the softness of the bed, my heavy eyelids, and the soothing voice of my father or mother as they conjured stories from the air or sang lullabies. As I grew so did my love of tales and I would often find myself, without intention, the storyteller when gathered with friends around the campfire. Looking back I can see that stories were everywhere in my life: in friendships, in family history, in warnings and reprimands and of course in falling in love. I loved nothing quite so much as to listen and become lost in a tale, or to sit, pen in hand, and create my own.

In 2001, after reading my writings, a friend suggested that I had a strong narrative voice and that I should consider storytelling as a possible career. I had never thought of it as a profession and enthusiastically set about finding out about it. I found Liz Weir, a storyteller based in Co Antrim, Northern Ireland, and she invited me to shadow her for three days. I took her up on the offer and watched her work around Northern Ireland in places ranging from Montessori schools to libraries. I came to realise that storytelling was a profession, but wasn't sure if it was for me.

Two years later I met John Moriarty, a walking living breathing library of tales. John is a modern mystic, and he infected everyone around him with his sense of wonder at the world. He did so through the power of stories. He wove his stories together in such a delicate tapestry that they enveloped the audience's minds with an easy brilliance and then they unfolded before us in breath-taking splendour. It was there in that audience, listening to John recapture the old love epic of Diarmuid and Grainne that I became aware of a deep power behind stories: their ability to transform us at a fundamental level. My passion for tales was rekindled.

As I began telling stories, friends asked me to teach them storytelling. I refused, offering instead to create a space in which we could all tell, and all listen. In 2006 I set about creating a Story Night, where first time and long time storytellers could tell tales in a friendly atmosphere. So we gathered on cushions around the candle-flame, our hearts in our mouths, as tales of ghosts and ghouls, bizarre family histories and ancient epics were spun and respun. But the number of people gathering grew exponentially, and eventually we graduated to a local theatre for the first public story night. Its success was undeniable and the event has been running every month since.

From then on there was no denying my passion or purpose. I was a natural storyteller, I loved it, I relished it, and now I had somewhere to play with it. Work came flowing in from libraries and schools and festivals, and I found myself working at it full time. I have never looked back.

The beauty of what I do lies in its simplicity and in its universality. Almost every culture in the world has stories at its foundation. Every psyche has, at its root, the stories that shaped it. This means that everyone loves a good story. So more often than not, half of my work is done for me already, and I am met with faces full of expectation and excitement at the chance to sit back, relax and be immersed in stories.

I was extraordinarily well supported by local librarians at Galway City Library, especially in the Children's Department. However work soon led down more unpredictable roads. Invitations came in from heritage centres, arts centres, children's festivals, book weeks, bookshops, universities, refugee support groups, youth at risk groups, teachers, children's theatre groups and elsewhere. I ran a storytelling week at Project '06, a Festival of Local Arts in Galway, which led to a creative partnership with fellow storyteller and writer Rab Swannock Fulton. The richness of this collaboration has led to many successful storytelling projects and ventures, including the online archive of our work at the website www.storytellersunlimited.com sponsored by Arts Council of Ireland's Deis Traditional Arts fund. One the many interesting projects Rab and I do together is the Storytelling in Schools Programme that we began in December 2006 and have run successfully for the past two years – of which more later.

In 2007 I was awarded a grant by Social Entrepreneurs Ireland, a grant that allowed me to develop an idea called *Community Storytelling*. Social Entrepreneurs believed in me totally and gave me unstinting support and access to their massive social and business network. Their encouragement and unfaltering belief helped to push me forward, it gave me breathing space and the time to develop my Intergenerational Project and another project due in Autumn 2008.

The purpose behind Community Storytelling is to build bridges between marginalised members of society and mainstream society. It also aims to give people a space for their voices to be heard, which is vital to this reconnection. Part one of Community Storytelling was called *The Intergenerational project*. It sought to connect two age groups: the elderly and teenagers, in the hope of creating greater and deeper communication between them.

Rab and I worked with both groups over a period of seven weeks. With the teenagers we concentrated on the craft and technique of storytelling, while with the elderly we worked on memory, openness and celebration of story. After four weeks we brought the groups together – with great success. Then they were reunited after seven weeks so the teenagers could perform stories adapted from the memories of the old folks. The outcome far exceeded our hopes. There was a serious shift in attitude by each group towards the other, and increased confidence and self expression in the teenagers. Part of the inspiration for this programme came from a similar programme run in Lisbon by professional storyteller Sofia Maul, who works with the Contabandistas Storytelling Troupe. We took inspiration from her work and adapted it to our environment. The projects demonstrate that storytelling has the power to nurture and develop good relationships in society.

The simple gathering of friends that grew into the monthly Story Night is still going strong. It has the youngest people in the country to be involved in swapping stories, and celebrated its second birthday in July 2008. The basic idea is to create a communal space where anyone can come and listen to a story or tell one. Attending is cheap and by donation so as not to exclude anyone. A sign of its health and strength is that every month there are regular attendees and also new faces. There are usually anywhere from 20 to 40 people, aged between 18 and 60. The stories range from the personal to the mythological, from local folklore to the anecdotal. It is always a thoroughly enjoyable and surprising evening – one never knows what one will hear. I consider it one of my best projects to date.

Our Storytelling in Schools project, however, is one of the most satisfying of the various types of storytelling work we do. Devised and directed by Rab and myself, the project is funded by the Access office at the National University of Ireland in Galway. The Access office works with students from families that have little or no experience of third level education. Through helping children and school leavers develop personally by building their self esteem, confidence, communication skills and social behaviour, the Access Office raises aspirations, and many of the students are now studying as postgraduates at the National University of Ireland in Galway. We were asked to work as part of their Sports for Success programme (thereafter renamed the *Uni for You* programme). This programme works with primary school children, offering events (originally sporting events) held at the local university. We were asked to run a six week storytelling programme for 6th class (11-12 year olds) that would culminate in a storytelling performance given by all the participants during the Muscailt Arts Festival at NUIG.

Rab and I had never given workshops on such a scale. We considered it a wonderful opportunity as it gave us time with the children to develop their skills and give them time to practise before the performance. Using the model Jack Zipes describes in his book *Creative Storytelling* (1995), we set about devising a six week programme that would develop the children's natural storytelling ability, confidence, self expression and imagination.

Zipes breaks down his own school programmes in a step by step, lesson by lesson way that we found easy to understand and follow. The scope of his work and breadth of his understanding is inspirational and gave us ideal parameters to work within. We adapted his model, drawing from our own experiences and ideas; this allowed us to synthesise our creativity with his. The end result was six weeks that were dedicated to engage, stimulate and develop the minds of the children.

The idea was to let the children perform a story of their own creation at Muscailt. We were aware that the quieter children would be reticent and the boisterous children would be exuberant, so our challenge was to make sure everyone got their chance to speak and everyone had the confidence to express themselves in public. The schools we worked in were in the Uni for You programme because of their 'disadvantaged' status, as they are in working class areas with low university application rates. We were made welcome by the teachers of all three schools. They felt that not only did it allow the children to shine in a non-academic setting, but that creating stories developed the children's confidence in ways that improved their literacy skills.

Rab and I began the programme with high hopes. Some of the children knew us from previous work, and this established an easygoing atmosphere from the start. We began by outlining what we planned on doing, and told a few stories. We found that the children were quick to engage in debate right away about stories and the possible alternatives to what had been presented. Their willingness to engage proved to be a great strength and enriched their story-telling performances at the end of the programme.

Over the six weeks we walked the children through the basic structures of fairy tales and tall tales, giving them weekly homework tasks of creating or finding a story. The basic structure of the programme was as follows:

- What is storytelling? Demonstration and discussion on stories, their meanings. Criticism encouraged.
- Breaking down the fairy tale – how to reconstruct your own tale.
- Tall tales – creating your own stories from a combination of the real and the surreal.
- Developing the stories – working on narrative, characters, plots and conclusions.
- Developing the telling – working on voice, eye contact and confidence in delivery.
- Preparing for the show at Muscailt Arts Festival, National University of Ireland, Galway.

We encouraged positive criticism from the children right from the start. Positive criticism entails critiquing the story and not the person. It is about suggesting how to improve a story rather than saying what you didn't like about it. This appraisal was well received and, although it took a while for the children to learn how to receive criticism, in the end we found it a very useful tool in developing the children's stories and also their ability for critical thinking. It allowed them to gain greater understanding of the structure of the story, rather than just saying that something was good or bad, boring or exciting. They had to apply their critique to characters or plotlines, to conclusions or the problems inherent within the stories.

In both the years we ran this project we found a tendency for the children to be drawn to the gorier stories, and to create stories about violence and blood-shed. This could be due partly to what they are exposed to on television and computer games, and partly to the natural lure for all children of the scary story. Rab and I have learned through the practice of giving the workshops that there are a few ways to deal with it:

- Do not ignore or prohibit the use of violence, as this only encourages the children to want to do it more

- Lead by example: do not use stories where violence or bloodshed are the main theme or solution

- Challenge the use of the violence in the tale: if a child makes a choice to destroy the monster in their story by violent means such as a bazooka or machine gun, ask them how the character came by the weapon. If indeed the monster is so scary that it must be gotten rid of, we found that if we challenged the children to explain how their heroes got hold of weapons or powers to overcome the villains, they often come up with wonderfully imaginative alternatives

- As Jack Zipes (1995) suggests, one can create a session of tales that encourage discussion about alternative endings to the violence or destruction that typifies fairy tales. Opening up the topic of violence allows children to engage openly with their ideas.

In one workshop that worked really well, we gave the children a story with no ending. Here is a synopsis:

> Betsy loved science fiction. From the time she could read she devoured everything she could from that genre. She read so much sci fi that she wanted to be a member of the Intergalactic Space Guards when she grew up. Regardless of what her parents and teachers said about this 'fantasy', Betsy's belief would not be shaken. On her way to the shops one day, she saw a bright light in the sky and watched as an alien craft landed, and aliens emerged from it. They took Betsy prisoner and demanded to be taken to the leader of the planet or they threatened to release a deadly fart that would wipe out the whole planet.

The story stops there and we asked the children to create a suitable ending. First came a barrage of ideas around violence, using weapons the children would know about from television and video games. But after being challenged on how Betsy would suddenly turn out to have a gun, the children began to come up with imaginative alternatives. Here are three of them:

- Thanks to all her reading, Betsy knows these aliens are pretty stupid, and also that they are allergic to water. She tricks them into letting her go and buy a water pistol, and then she threatens them with it until they leave the planet.

- Betsy agrees to take the aliens to the leader and leads them out of the space craft. She says she is walking them to her leader but, knowing they are allergic to water, she leads them over a covered swimming pool. The weight of the aliens forces them to sink below the cover and all five are dissolved in the water that is toxic to them.

- Betsy agrees to take the aliens to her leader, but she stalls, leading them on a wild goose chase around the planet. This gives the Intergalactic Space Guards time to arrive and arrest the aliens. Before they leave the guards congratulate Betsy on her good work and ask her if she would consider joining up.

During the couple of years of doing this programme, we have learned that it was vital to focus the children's creativity into one area. When we gave homework that was too broad – 'Bring a story to class next week' – many of the children faltered and brought nothing in. When we were specific, giving a title, a genre or an unfinished story, we found they rose readily to the challenge. But there is also a danger in being too restrictive. We gave one class specific elements that they had to use in a story and the children's creativity was choked by the narrowness of the exercise. The stories produced were obviously not stories that the children liked or were proud of. Setting exercises which have parameters that are loose enough to allow for much creativity, yet narrow enough to bring a focused intention to the story produced, is a delicate matter.

Although six weeks is a splendid amount of time to work with children, we have realised that it is essential not to cram in too much. It is better to use a single genre of stories to teach all the basic information needed about structure and creativity. We have found fairy tales or tall tales work very well. In the first year we tried to pack in too much information, and although the children enjoyed themselves and produced wonderful stories, we realise from our experience that focusing in on one genre allows the children to acquire greater depth of learning. As this project will, we hope, continue, it will no doubt change constantly as we learn more from our engagement with children.

My work continues to challenge me and bring me to new and interesting places. Storytelling is an exceptionally wonderful way to meet beautiful people all over the world who share this passion for tales. It has led me to encounters with inspiring people who influence and change the shape of my life. John Moriarty once said that the greatest state for the human being to be in was a state of wonder. It is a state, he said, which we often connect with childhood, because children, on account of their innocence, can live in that state a great deal of the time. My hope is that with my work I can help people find that state of wonder, when the world is new and beautiful and surprising all over again. A state of being that allows us new eyes and a refreshed spirit.

Christine McMahon: giving away stories

Interview by George Murphy

Christine McMahon has an international reputation as a teller of traditional folk-tales and stories based in the industrial past of Lancashire and Yorkshire. She is an energetic organiser and participant in community events, especially with younger people, and a regular performer at the Shaggy Dog Storytellers Club.

GM: Please explain how you became a storyteller and tell us about some of the highlights in your storytelling career.

CM: My background is in teaching drama and psychology, and this led to drama therapy. Long before that though, I had a dream about finding stories so when I heard of the storytelling club I went. The club has been the thread that has held everything together since that moment. Three of the highlights of my storytelling career have been: working in prisons, having international visitors and telling stories in far-off places.

GM: You don't spend all your time storytelling. I understand, though, that you manage to make links to storytelling in your other career? Can you tell us about your other work?

CM: I work in the justice system – in restorative justice – helping victims and offenders to come together to find a way forward and helping young people to face up to what they have done. Storytelling has a twofold role: one is in helping people to tell *their* story, to find resolution to the conflict. The other is telling stories to young people who feel they are failures, to encourage, entertain and share.

GM: As you know, this book is focusing on storytelling in primary schools. I know you have done a lot of work in schools. Could you tell us about some of the most memorable work?

CM: This is what springs to mind. Firstly, I love seeing children react when I tell them back the stories they have created with me – they can't believe what they have made! It's also great to see children gaining the confidence to perform. I once worked with children who had not yet developed language properly and it was fascinating hearing a whole group of them apparently speaking – and understanding – a private language that sounded like gobbledegook to me. They loved stories and listened beautifully.

GM: From your point of view, what are the characteristics of a successful school visit? What are your requirements and what do you expect from teachers?

CM: There are several things I would list. I'll write them down for you. (*Christine scribbled down the following list*):

- Prior discussion of the agreed aims. Some teachers require entertainment and some want literacy development and some want development of oral skills
- A cup of tea on arrival!
- Teachers to participate in the session
- No censorship of stories and types of tales – for instance some teachers say 'no witches, no magic, nothing scary'
- Freedom to be creative, but support from the teachers who will trust that I know what I am doing ... ie don't interfere too much!

GM: Have you any advice you would like to pass on to teachers about their storytelling? And what strategies do you recommend for helping young children to develop as tellers of tales?

CM: Tips ... all teachers should go on a course! Put down the book and have a go! I've found that teachers who are confident with their own oral storytelling give children confidence in theirs. Time is everything – it's really worth investing in this and incorporating stories into all subjects.

GM: I have seen you tell a variety of tales, but you especially seem to favour humorous folktales based in the north of England. Do you have some favourite stories you use with children?

CM: I love the one about the baby who wants apple juice and sends parents and siblings down to the cellar – the story grabs all the little ones. I got it from a New Zealand teller, Mary Kippenberger. I also love an African tale about a rabbit that finds a monster in its house. In my version, it is of course a Yorkshire rabbit, and the monster is escaping from the rain! It is about fearsome things not being as bad as you think!

GM: I know several variations on that theme. I've seen it in a reading scheme based on an African hunting tale. There's also a version in Betty Rosen's book that I call 'The monster over the mountain'. There's a writer-illustrator called Tony Ross who has a story where the monster is an alien, but he turns out to be much smaller than the boy he is trying to terrorise. Finally, Chris: I'll put you on the spot: what do you see as the value of storytelling in education?

CM: I'd say that story is a thread that holds everything together. Stories can carry information ... help children to hold the information in a way that the brain can retain it. Stories also offer hope. Imagination can't flourish without stories. I believe every child needs stories to survive.

My favourite quote is: 'When stories come to you, learn to care for them and learn to give them away where they are needed. Sometimes people need stories more than food to stay alive.' That's from Aaron Shepard's storytelling page on the internet.

Shaping and sharing – how to tell a tale

Maggie Power

Maggie describes how she encourages students to tell stories to children and how she approaches the task. She describes the techniques for telling, shaping and sharing a tale.

> The process of learning how to tell a story is a process of empowerment. We all want to narrate our lives, but very few of us have been given the techniques and insights that can help us form plots to reach our goals. We need to learn strategies of narration when we are young in order to grasp that we can become our own narrators, the storytellers of our lives. (Zipes, 1995)

Jack Zipes captures the essence of what is important to me about becoming a teller of tales. Teachers and children need the empowerment that comes from forming their own stories about the minutiae of their daily existence or from retelling stories from other places and times. Students can develop their own ability to tell tales in the hope that they will nurture that confidence in children.

Students as storytellers

In our work with the students to prepare them for their work with children, we give them time in college to share and then shape their tales. They have opportunities to craft the tale, and in many instances to assemble props to help in the telling. Using props helps provide security, offering a pattern to the young teller. Old lampshades have been turned into mountains for a Chinese tale. Card is made into puppets. Some commercially prepared puppets can support a storytelling or they can be made from old – but clean – socks or whatever is to hand. It is for the students to decide.

The visit to a local school allows for interaction and small group contact. The students meet at the school before the school day starts and are welcomed by a senior member of staff with drinks and biscuits. They are then taken in groups of four or five to the classrooms. The children know they are coming and are waiting expectantly.

The selected stories allow each group of children to be told four or five stories within the session. The students are often nervous. How will they manage in the nursery? Will the older children be bored or the younger ones distracted?

Ten minutes after the tellings have started, a walk around the school and a look through a window or peep around a door confirms that the students' fears were groundless. Everywhere is a buzz of interest and enjoyment. Sharing and telling a story in an interactive way draws a response from the children and leaves them with tales both old and new. And the students gain satisfaction and discover the power of telling tales to children.

But how do I tell a story?

- I dress for the part. I have a storytelling skirt – black but decorated with swirls of vivid colour. It is long but comfortable and easy to move around in. I have a necklace that is made of buttons and matches the colours in the skirt. I say it is my storytelling skirt and I know as many stories as there are buttons in my necklace! I ask the children 'Do you know that many stories?'

- I introduce myself to the children, whether it is a class or a hall full. I tell them who I am and why I have come into their school. I want to show them very quickly that this will be different from the work that happens day in and day out in schools. I do the same if it is a large group of students at college; I introduce myself and set the scene.

- I explain that I have come to tell stories. I talk about hearing how clever they are at telling and listening to stories themselves. I always focus at first on what they already know and how those stories have got into their heads.

- I talk about needing help – first from everyone, to put sound effects with the story, a little like the volume control on the television. I hold both my hands together in front of me and say 'This is no sound at all – that is when it is so quiet in the room that if you pulled a hair from your head and dropped it you could hear it land on the carpet'. I then part my hands and move them upwards saying 'This is some sound' – the more I open and raise my hands the more sound there needs to be, until when both arms are held up above my head that is as much noise as they can make. We practise the sound of the wind rustling through the trees early in the morning. It can sometimes take a few goes for everyone to focus but the effect is always very powerful, be they a group of six year olds or 100 postgraduate students in a lecture theatre.

- I introduce other sounds, sounds that relate to the story we will tell. When there are footsteps, I hold my hands flat in front of me and move them up and down. The children can copy this in the air or tap their knees or a flat surface. It is easy to alter the pace and strength of the steps so you go from creeping to running but I keep everyone involved. Other sounds – doors opening, gates creaking, rain falling – create an atmosphere. All can be introduced and orchestrated. The sound orchestra, demanding as it does involvement and concentration, quickly sets the mood I require and it develops a cooperative spirit in the group.

- Then I outline what the story will be about and identify characters. I say I will be looking for children who would like to assist and be one of those characters. What's important is for the children to know that at no point will they be exposed or feel vulnerable or lost for words. If I need a giant I ask for volunteers or I ask all the children and adults to sit as one at a click of the fingers or bang of the drum. Whenever I am unsure I can involve other adults but most of the time I follow my own feelings about whom to involve. I once chose a child who was bursting with enthusiasm. As he came forward there was a collective sigh from the adults in the room. They told me afterwards that he had a pronounced stutter and they were anxious for him. I had no expectation of this and he did all I asked him to and was a loud, clear and determined giant throughout. I draw on the selected characters as I tell the story but they echo my telling of the story.' And the giant said, 'Where is the little girl? I want to eat her.' As I say this, I turn to the child or touch their shoulder and they repeat the words – in character.

- At other points in the story all the children may echo my words ... 'And he was worried' ... Whatever it is, it can be repeated in many ways by the children, thus securing their involvement and enjoyment. With children who are developing confidence in using spoken English this is a valuable way of sustaining their engagement while also enabling them to use and share language that may otherwise still be beyond them.

- ▨ Another useful tool for engaging the audience is to get them to hold both hands under their chin and then pull them up over their face – rather like opening and closing a blind. With each movement up or down they present a change of expression or mood: Now show me a happy face. What makes you feel like that? Now a frightened face. The possibilities are endless.
- ▨ Sound, however it is provided, can greatly strengthen the storytelling. I use a boran but also instruments that I think suit a particular tale. And I also use other items from the room I am in: a box full of pencils; a ruler banged against a table, and many more.

All these are only suggestions. With any storytelling or sharing, what matters most is that the teller feels at ease with whatever devices they introduce to draw in the children. I suggest to my students that they try using one strategy in their telling of a tale, then evaluate it in the light of how it engaged the audience or strengthened the telling and whether the strategy felt right for them.

With practice comes confidence and the ability to be flexible in the telling and sharing. Storytellers need to think on their feet and constantly adjust; sometimes more sounds are required, sometimes less. They need an instinctive sense of what will enhance children's enjoyment and involvement. The moment comes where you can hold the attention and enjoyment of the group in the palm of your hand, as a good actor on stage feels that everyone is with them. It's magic!

But for the children to be powerful storytellers they need above all to become bringers of magic into their own lives, into their classrooms, and into their homes. Storytelling is hugely empowering. Here I rest my case for the need to develop powerful storytellers amongst the children as well as the adults.

How children help teachers to tell stories

George Murphy

George describes how he tells stories, focusing on a Scottish tale he told to members of the Shaggydog Story Tellers Club.

he best stories are spell-binding, and the spell works best on children. Take a story like *Little Dog Turpie*, an old Scottish story that was carried across the sea by emigrants to America and Australasia. In early versions the protagonists live in a house made of hemp stalks close to salt marshes, the marginal lands that form the backdrop to many ancient tales featuring dark and malevolent spirits. The story has a quality of dark humour, shared by tales such as *Der Strewelpetter* by Heinrich Hoffman or *Gashlycrumb Tinies* in the illustrated rhymes of Edward Gorey. Except that this magical tale has a happy ending.

I told this story at the Shaggydog Storytellers club: a roomful of storytellers, club members (used to seeing professional performers), and a good crowd of parents and children. The ebullient m.c introduced me by announcing that this was the first story I had told at the club. I found myself walking to the front, glad of the generous applause, but thinking to myself, why are my legs walking in this direction when they should be running the other way? But the children helped me.

The younger children had threatened to disrupt earlier stories, becoming noisy and fidgety or wandering out to stand at the front and look back to wave at their parents in the audience – to the consternation of some of the performers. Fortunately, as a former infant school teacher, I could still call on the big theatrical voice that early years' teachers use on such occasions: 'I'm SO glad to see so many children here, because in this story I need some children who are good at barking!'

There followed twenty seconds of growls, barks and howls that, thankfully, subsided when I held up my hand. I congratulated them and said that this would be the signal for them to stop barking when I told my story. So far so good: it was good to have the kids on my side. However, to get safely through my debut performance I wanted to enlist the adults too. 'And children,' I said, looking directly into the upturned, wide-eyed faces of the children at the front, 'I'll let you into a secret: adults like barking too! So if you are sitting next to an adult and they forget to bark, give them a little nudge as a reminder.'

Then we had a short practice. 'The hero of this story is called Little Dog Turpie. When I say, 'Little Dog Turpie barked SO loud...' I want you all to start barking.'

So they all barked on cue. I was particularly struck by the volume and enthusiasm of the men in the audience.

I had chosen this tale because it had always worked when I told it to my own kids, who knew the value of a good, scary tale. But I was worried that some parents might think it was *too* frightening. So I explained things to the children, knowing that the parents would be listening too. 'This is a very frightening story...'

Whoops, one little lad looked genuinely terrified.

'There are Hobyahs in this story! So if you tell this story to an adult, perhaps to your grandma, please say to them: it's alright grandma, there aren't any Hobyahs left these days.'

The boy nodded, a grave, responsible expression on his face. This would be my life-line; I could check how my story was going by watching the children's faces. Like most adults, I've loved watching the rapt attention and spontaneous reactions of children during a puppet show or an exciting, funny or moving film or play. As a teacher I had always relished it when I saw that my class were caught up in the world of a story I was telling or reading to them. So I began:

> A little old man and a little old woman and a little girl lived in a turnip house with Little Dog Turpie. One night, the Hobyahs came.

Now I pulled a face and distorted my voice and half crouched as I paraded up and down.

> 'Hobyah, hobyah, hobyah' they said! 'Tear down the turnip house, eat the old man and eat the old woman, put the girl in a bag and away we go!'

> But Little Dog Turpie barked so loud...

Mercifully, the whole audience came in on cue, sounding like an angrier version of the RSPCA pound. Just as quickly they responded to my signal to fall silent again.

> ...that all the hobyahs ran away. Next morning, the little old man said, 'Little Dog Turpie barked SO loud...'

Well, didn't they give it full volume now? And this time they were harder to stop, but that became part of the humour.

> ... 'that I could neither sleep, nor slumber.'

> So he went downstairs and he cut off Little Dog Turpie's tail!

Now there came groans of admonishment from some adults in the audience – enjoying their pantomime role – but not from the children, who are used to the severe chastisements of fantasy and fairy tales. I wasn't expecting the adult reaction but I was ready next time. For each time the Hobyahs came the little dog scared them away and in the morning the old man took his axe to the dog and chopped off his legs and finally his head and the adults all groaned again. And they probably thought, 'Where is this story going?'

Well, the next night the Hobyahs returned and they couldn't find the little old man – who had hidden under his bed – and they should have eaten the little old woman, but I backed down on that. Next morning, there was no sign of the little girl, or the old woman. So the old man went to talk to Little Dog Turpie. With more confidence, I could have played this part of the story with mock pathos, which might have appealed to the adults in the audience. But I was more concerned with my child listeners.

> Fortunately, that was a magic time. And the little old man soon sewed Little Dog Turpie together again.

Then I surprised myself by ad libbing:

> Except the first time, he didn't get it quite right and he sewed a leg on where Little Dog Turpie's tail should have been. But Little Dog Turpie barked so loud...

Once more the canine cacophony erupted and I struggled to muzzle it – especially the howls from the large, elderly gentleman in the second row.

> ...that the old man had to undo his error. But soon Little Dog Turpie was all back together again.

So the old man and the dog set off and they walked all day. And as I describe this, I remember to say that they didn't meet the hobyahs because the hobyahs only came out at night, which was quite an important detail and I was glad I remembered it in time. Because as the sun starts to set, the little old man and Little Dog Turpie come to the mouth of a cave and there's a black bag hanging from a hook and something is squirming around in the bag. Then they can hear the little girl crying. They open the bag and – in my version – they are delighted to find that the little old woman is there too (because the hobyahs had eaten too well to eat her up last night). So the girl and the old woman get out and the old man puts Little Dog Turpie in the bag and sews it up.

Now just before concluding the tale, I should point out that the little girl's ordeal could have been made grimmer. Mary Smallwood from Devon has told me a version of the tale that she told her children more than forty years ago. Mary didn't think the hobyahs were really so terrible (she also told Hoffman's cautionary tales to her children). She told me that the world wouldn't be such a bad place if the worst thing in it were hobyahs. In Mary's version, the hobyahs delighted, when they had captured the little girl, in jumping up at the bag shouting 'Look me! Look me!' in their little hobyah voices. I think children would enjoy that and the puddle of tears that the girl made on the floor beneath the bag, because it ratchets up the tension before the denouement, but these elements were missing from my account.

> So when darkness came, the hobyahs all gathered around the bag and they chanted, 'Hobyah, hobyah, hobyah: eat up the old woman, eat up the little girl. Hobyah, hobyah, hobyah!
>
> But Little Dog Turpie barked SO loud...

This time the audience let rip. I indulged them for a while. Finally, I raised my hand:

> ...that all the hobyahs ran away. But Little Dog Turpie ran after them...

The boy at the front of the audience caught my eye again and I looked directly at him.

> And he ate them all up, every single one.

Nearly done, and the story had come full circle. I looked up but didn't see my audience.

> And that's why there are no more hobyahs left.

And I bowed.

So I did manage to overcome my fear. I made my way to my seat. I was delighted with the applause and equally pleased when the m.c ended the evening by saying that the audience deserved a special treat: not only could they applaud themselves for being a marvellous audience, but they could bark as well. I went home feeling very relieved because at that time I still felt more comfortable as a teacher than a performer.

The Crick Crack Club website makes a distinction between *performance storytelling* to a large group and *fireside* storytelling. The latter involves fewer listeners – who are usually all known by the teller – in familiar, intimate settings. Perhaps classroom storytelling is closer to the hearth than the stage. But my little performance reminded me of the power of stories told to children, when their honest, open faces react to the twists and turns and thrills of a well told tale.

Part 4
Working with students

A module to grow with

Maggie Power

Education is a journey, an adventure from which both the child and the teacher are equipped to move forward. Maggie looks at how students are equipped with knowledge and experience to move into classrooms.

The School of Teaching, Health and Care at Bradford College offers a module that explores the nature and place of narrative in the primary classroom. The module is studied during the second year of the course and is compulsory for language specialists on the four year BA QTS. It is also offered to students on an Education Studies degree who plan to work in various educational settings: in the arts, tourism and leisure centres, museums, schools or careers advice offices. The ability to tell historical, traditional and contemporary stories is a useful accomplishment for them all. They also spend time crafting a written retelling of a traditional tale.

We start the course by introducing traditional tales. A quick audit of knowledge during the first session usually confirms that most if not all know the stories of Cinderella, Red Riding Hood, Aladdin and others from their childhood. These stories are familiar to students with family roots in Europe or the Indian sub-continent. *Kitabes*, simple books written in Urdu, contain most of these well known traditional tales. We have found that the only students who have no knowledge of this heritage are those from mainland China. They had never heard of Hansel and Gretel and didn't even know which character was the boy and which the girl. Further discussion, however, revealed several Chinese tales that covered the same themes as the Indo-European tales.

In the first part of the module we try to immerse the students in stories from around the world and from different times and places. We start with Angela

Carter's *Virago Book of Fairy Tales* (1990) then select stories from collections of tales from Africa, India, Pakistan and forgotten tales from the British Isles. We try to provide variety whilst making connections between different traditions. We also model the telling of tales. Whilst expanding and developing a repertoire of tales we look at *Anansi* stories, with their roots in both Africa and America and the Caribbean and consider how these trickster tales were dispersed. We compare stories from all over the world that have similar patterns to *Cinderella* or *Red Riding Hood* and set students the task of investigating and trying to account for their similarities and differences.

The expansion of their knowledge and movement away from the limits of their own childhood experience is important. It will enable the students to move into their own work as teachers, trainers and instructors with more than the Disneyfied version of these ancient examples of world culture in their repertoire.

Students are shown the characteristic features of myth, fable and fairy – or wonder – tale and asked to look again at their reading and categorise what they have read. At this stage we ask them to select a tale they like, one they feel they would be able to tell and share with children in a local primary school.

Following immersion comes the telling: the ability to share a tale with a group of children. We have developed and maintained links with inner city Bradford schools where the majority of the children have parents or grandparents who came from Pakistan. For some children English is their second language, for others it is their main language but they also use Punjabi to communicate with family members. Grandparents looked after some of them while their parents were at work before they began school, and they spent most of the day conversing in Punjabi.

Students decide what tale they want to share in the classroom, then indicate which age group they would like to work with. College staff work with the link teacher to arrange a programme that offers variety to the children and wherever possible meets students' requests about the age group they want to tell their story to. During college sessions the students develop their skills in telling and sharing a tale. They are encouraged to make props to support their story. Bilingual students are encouraged to find ways in which they can introduce a range of languages into their telling

Students from other European institutions who come to study with us under the Erasmus programme often choose to take the module. They too are encouraged to use their home language in their tellings.

The ability to communicate, to maintain the interest of a small group of people and give them pleasure, is a skill to be developed in all who want to work in the classroom. For some students it is an immense challenge and something they have to work over time to develop. For some it involves talking to a mirror. One student even practised by talking to her dog.

The time in school flies by. After being welcomed, the students are allocated to classrooms or spaces where the children await them. The older ones know what to expect and all are eager. The books and worksheets are put away and the children are keen to listen but also to contribute. They can be asked questions, given a chorus to repeat, offered puppets to hold, all in a small group where the storytellers can see and sustain the children's interest. The teacher stays in the room and also enjoys the stories as they unfold or are held in the air.

The students know they have to hold the interest of the children for the duration of their tale but also that they have to be able to chat and engage them until most have finished sharing their stories. Then it is up and away – either the children move on to the next storyteller or the students move to the next group. Generally the children get to hear four or five tales in the course of the visit. The children are then moved to share others they know from home or have heard in school. No link is made with writing – this needs to be an exercise in pure enjoyment for the children, a time for enrichment, an offering without strings. And it is justified for that alone.

Recently we have added another task for students: they tell a prepared story to a group of fellow students and staff as part of their final assessment.

Before presenting their own written tales, the students look at how stories change over time. We consider the importance of the Grimm brothers' stories in Germany and the collections of Perrault in France. When considering the transformation of spoken folktales into written fairy tales, the students think about:

- who had control?
- who selected the stories?
- what was retained and what omitted?

These matters are important because what is included in the written version was often the work of the collector and the editor and not that of the original storyteller.

Stories given to children in earlier times can be contrasted with what children are told today. Students and teachers could ask themselves certain questions:

- are we giving the children experience of a variety of stories from a number of cultures and backgrounds?
- are boys featured in a range of roles?
- are the girls always pretty and voiceless and acquiescent?
- do the girls always need to win their prince?

The challenge for the students is to write a tale that is their own, a tale they can create from what they now know of the patterns and norms of traditional or wonder tales. What could they add to the world of tales for the enjoyment of children and adults? As well as affording the satisfaction that comes from creation, the written tale is a vehicle to demonstrate understanding. The story is accompanied by a commentary within which the students can identify common features and patterns in their story that relate to what is definably a traditional or wonder tale.

Princess Sonia: the ordinary princess

Shabana Kausar

Princess Sonia, the ordinary princess
– a tale by Shabana Kausar

Once upon a time, in the polluted city of Bradford, lived Princess Sonia. Actually Sonia was not a princess at all. Her mother and father called her that because she was their only child – so very precious to them. Princes Sonia was not particularly beautiful. In fact she was not beautiful at all. Her black hair was neither straight nor curly, her brown eyes neither twinkly nor dull. Princess Sonia was the most ordinary looking girl in the world.

One day, a terrible event struck Princess Sonia's life. Her mother was crushed under a heavily loaded shopping trolley in Morrison's and died. Princess Sonia was very sad and cried a lot. She would never be able to pass a supermarket again without thinking of her poor mother drawing her last breath in the frozen chips section.

Princess Sonia's father was also quite sad, but he recovered quickly. One evening, he sat Sonia down and announced that he was remarrying. Not long after, the stepmother arrived. As stepmothers go, she was fairly standard: angelic outside, evil inside. She hated Princess Sonia and convinced Sonia's father to get rid of her. As the social workers would not have approved of them locking Princess Sonia in a scary dungeon, they decided to find Princess Sonia a husband. They did not have to look very far. For Princess Sonia had a cousin who was so ugly and horrid that nobody wanted to marry him. Princess Sonia did not want to marry him either. She did not want to marry him at all.

As it turned out, she had no choice. When she told her father and stepmother about not wanting to marry her cousin, they slapped her very hard, locked her in her room and told her that if she did not marry him she would die. Poor Princess Sonia! She was extremely frightened. And so, feeling helpless, she married her cousin.

Princess Sonia did not like her husband, Prince Charmless. She did not like him at all. Both Prince Charmless and his wrinkly mother were very cruel to Princess Sonia. They made her cook chapatti and chips every day. She had to clean their semi-detached house until it gleamed. She was not allowed out; she was not allowed any visitors.

One day, Princess Sonia was very poorly. When Prince Charmless returned from a day of doing nothing, she was too ill to polish his boots. This enraged Prince Charmless. He flew at Princess Sonia in a fit of fury and tried to kill her. At first, Princess Sonia was afraid. In fact, she was petrified. But the sight of Prince Charmless charging at her, sweating and with his eyes bulging, made Princess Sonia brave. Enough is enough, she thought.

'If you come near me,' she shouted, 'I will rip you into a million pieces and feed you to the neighbour's cat! I am leaving you forever, Prince Charmless, don't you dare try to follow me!'

'I-I-I-I won't.' stammered Prince Charmless. He could see in his wife's eyes that she meant what she said and now *he* was afraid!

Princess Sonia rushed out of the house, pushing past Prince Charmless and his wrinkly mother. When she reached the gate, she stopped. Where would she go? What would she do? She looked towards her father's house. She could not go there; her stepmother would certainly not welcome her. She looked back at Prince Charmless's house. She could not return there either, for that life was unbearable.

She looked straight ahead, at the big polluted city of Bradford. Princess Sonia was not afraid at all. She had her savings account, with money her mother had left her. She had enough to live on. Perhaps she could go back to college, get a degree and get a good job. She had wanted to become a teacher a long time ago, she could do that now. Yes! That is what she would do! Princess Sonia skipped along. She did not have a husband, father, brother or son to look after her. 'But,' she thought, 'Why do I need a man?'

Why indeed? For Princess Sonia was a quick-witted and bright young woman. She did not need anyone to protect or provide for her. She could do that for herself. As long as she was brave and learnt from her mistakes, surely 'happy ever after' was not too far off?

Shabana submitted this story as part of her *Traditional Tales* assignment in 2006. Included is an extract from her theoretical essay. Shabana was awarded a first class degree in 2008 and is presently studying on the post graduate certificate of education to fulfil her dream of becoming a teacher.

Reflection on Princess Sonia

Barthes regarded fairytales as an example of the 'symbolic' sign, in which the text is encoded with polysemic messages (Culler, 1997). So, for example, the fairytale *Cinderella* could be viewed simply as a love story or it could be interpreted in a positive light as showing good overcoming evil, or in a negative light as an example of the powerful male asserting his authority over the passive female.

It is the latter meaning that has struck feminist commentators as being the dominant message in fairytales. Peet and Robinson (1997) assert that fairytales 'share wisdom' and underpin morals for the reader through their two dimensional characters. Caplan (1997) suggests, however, that when the dashing male rescues the beautiful but helpless female, the 'wisdom' that is being shared is that women are weak, incapable characters who need men to save them from cruelty, society at large and even themselves. This interpretation is valid for numerous fairytales, for instance *Sleeping Beauty* and *Snow White*.

The idea of female helplessness is a form of 'wisdom' that I did not want to convey through my fairytale. In light of the progress made in various strands of feminism, I do not feel that this message should be transmitted through popular forms of storytelling, in or out of educational institutions.

In *Princess Sonia: the ordinary princess*, I stayed within the accepted conventions of fairytale authoring, but steered well away from reinforcing gender stereotypes. Princess Sonia is neither beautiful nor endowed with extraordinary gifts. I chose the mundane, ordinary city of Bradford instead of a magic, faraway land, as the setting for the story; and a semi-detached house in place of a palace. There is no male hero to save Princess Sonia. She is the hero and she saves herself.

Feminist perspectives of literary criticism regard breaking stereotypes through fairytales and stories as a valuable way forward in achieving equality for women.

113

Caplan (1997) suggests that hegemonic rule is achieved in society through the use of books and literature in schools. 'Hegemony', as defined by Italian neo-Marxist theorist Gramsci, is the system of domination in society by one set of ideas. Feminists feel that men maintain patriarchal power hegemonically by persistently portraying woman as the weaker sex. Such books as fairytales, which are used widely in schools, condition both sexes into accepting their stereotypical roles.

Deliberately rejecting the stereotypes of most well-known fairytales inspired and shaped my own fairytale to its final form. But I did not want the message in the story to detract from the reader's enjoyment of it. Thus the story is a contemporary and amusing twist of the fairytale genre, with which both children and adults can engage. Different readers will decode different meanings and messages, as discussed by Barthes (1972).

Bradford (1996) notes that fairytales often portray images and characters that are consistent with the ideologies of the white community only, taking little account of other members of a culturally diverse society. A desire to represent aspects of ethnic minority life influenced the construction of my own fairytale, although I felt that the inclusion of too many politically correct ideas would not necessarily make a good story. Consequently, in *Princess Sonia*, I created a character that is not of any obvious ethnicity or cultural background. 'Sonia' is a name that is common to many cultures and her physical appearance is described in a manner that does not alienate any reader. I mention both 'chips' and 'chapattis' as an acknowledgement of the many different cultures living in 'the polluted city of Bradford'.

Thus, upon reflection, it would seem that fairytales do indeed have a vital role in society, both because of the enjoyment they provide and because of the deeper understanding they can bring to aspects of culture and society. The problem of constructing a tale the reader engages with is not as difficult as constructing a tale the reader also derives a meaningful message from, as I have discovered in writing my own tale. However, it is not impossible, as I have demonstrated in *Princess Sonia: the ordinary princess*. Once the readers, whatever their age, gender or cultural background, is thus engaged, they can sit back and access 'happily ever after', no matter how momentarily.

To conclude

We trust we have left you with stories that will resonate with you for some time. We remain confident in the power of narrative to be part of the affirmation of individuals and community and to enrich and extend the children in our schools.

We hope our readers will see the need to value the tales that are for telling in a range of languages and various cultural backgrounds and so support the creative work in schools and let in the storytellers.

We have every confidence in the teachers of today and the teachers of to-morrow to use narrative to enhance life, to open doors, to give children a reason to leave the room with their hands clasped over their ears to keep in a story and stop it flying away.

References

Ahlberg, A and J (2006) *The jolly postman, or other people's letters.* London: Puffin Books

Barrs, M (1994) *Genre theory: what's it all about?* Clevedon, Avon: OUP

Barthes, R (1972) *Mythologies.* London: Cape

Bartlett, F (1932) *Remembering: a study in experimental and social psychology.* Cambridge: Cambridge University Press

Bauman, R (1986) *Story, performance and event: contextual studies of oral narrative.* Cambridge: Cambridge University Press

Bearne, E (2000) *Where texts and children meet.* London: Routledge

Bettelheim, B (1976) *The uses of enchantment.* London: Thames and Hudson

Bradford, R (1997) *Introducing literary studies.* Hertfordshire: Harvester Wheatsheaf

Briggs, K (1977) *A sampler of British folk tales.* London and Henley: Routledge and Kegan Paul

Bunting, R (2000) *Teaching about language in the primary years.* Royston: UKRA mini-book series

Burgess, C *et al* (1971) *Understanding children's writing.* Harmondsworth: Penguin

Calvino, I (2000) *Italian folktales.* London: Penguin

Campbell, J (1993) *The hero with a thousand faces.* London: Fontana

Caplan, P (1996) *Feminist theory.* London: the Women's Press.

Carter, A (1990) *The Virago book of fairy tales.* London: Virago

Carter, A (2007) *Angela Carter's Book of Fairy Tales.* London: Virago

Carter, J (2001) *Creating Writers: a creative writing manual for schools.* London: Routledge Falmer

Colwell, E (1991) *Story Telling.* Oxford: Thimble Press

Corbett, P (2006) *The big book of storytelling into writing.* London: Clown Publishing

Crick crack club: ben@crickcrackclub.com and kate@crickcrackclub.com

Crossley-Holland, K (1989) *British folk tales: new versions.* London: Orchard

Crossley-Holland, K (2000) Different, but oh how like! In Cliff Hodges, G, Drummond, M.J and Styles, M *Tales, tellers and texts.* London: Cassell

Department for Education and Skills (2006) *Primary framework for literacy and mathematics.* Norwich: DfES Publications

Culler, J (1997) *An introduction to literary theory.* Oxford: Oxford University Press.

Department for Education and Skills (2003) *Excellence and enjoyment: a strategy for primary schools.* Norwich: DfES publications

Department for Education and Skills (2006) *Primary framework for literacy and mathematics.* Norwich: DfES Publications

DIECEC cities (1998) *Partnerships in education for citizenship and shared values regarding religion.* Bradford: Bradford Education

Education Department of Western Australia, (1996) *First steps: writing resource book.* Melbourne: Addison, Wesley, Longman

Egan, K (1988) *Teaching as storytelling: an alternative approach to teaching and the curriculum.* London: Routledge

Fox, C (1993) *At the very edge of the forest: the influence of literature on storytelling by children.* London: Cassell

Gorey, E (2005) *The gashlycrumb tinies.* Toronto: Pomegranate

Graham and Kelly (2007) *Reading under control: teaching reading in the primary school.* 3rd Edition. London: David Fulton

Grainger, T (1997) *Traditional Storytelling in the primary classroom.* Leamington Spa: Scholastic Ltd.

Halliday, M.A.K and Martin, J.R (1993) *Writing science: literacy and discursive power.* Sussex: Falmer

Hoffman, H (2008) *Der Strewelpeter or Shockheaded Peter.* Illinois: Bolchazy-Carducci

Labov, W (1972) *Language in the inner city: studies in the black English vernacular.* Philadelphia: University of Pennsylvania Press

Maul, S storyteller, Lisbon, Portugal Website: http://contabandistas.no.sapo.pt/

Peet, M and Robinson, D (1997) *The critical examination.* Leeds: Arnold – Wheaton.

Perera, K (1990) *Children's reading and writing: analysing classroom language.* London: Blackwell

Philip, N (1989) *The Cinderella story: the origins and variations of the story known as Cinderella.* London: Penguin

Piaget, J (1951) *Plays, dreams and imitation in childhood.* New York: Norton

Qualifications and Curriculum Authority (2004) *Religious education: the non-statutory national framework.* London: The QCA

Riley, J and Reedy, A (2000) *Developing writing for different purposes: teaching about genre in the early years.* London: Sage

Rosen, B. (1988) *And none of it was nonsense: The power of storytelling in school.* London: Mary Glasgow Publications

Rosen, B (1991) *Shapers and polishers.* London: Mary Glasgow

Rosen, C and Rosen, H (1973) *The language of primary school children.* Harmondsworth: Penguin

Ryan, P. *T3, Teachers Telling Tales.* Verbal arts centre, Derry/Londonderry, 2004 http://www.verbal artscentre.co.uk/EDUCATION/EDU_adult.htm

Shaggydog storytellers club: postmaster@shaggydogstorytellers.com

Stamboltzis, A and Pumfrey, P (2000) Reading across genres: a review of literature. *British journal of learning support Volume* 15 Issue 12 p95-99

Sunderland, M (2000) *Using story telling as a therapeutic tool with children.* Bicester: Winslow Press

Toye, N and Prendiville, F (2000) *Drama and traditional story for the early years.* London: Routledge

Swales, J M (1990) *Genre analysis: English in academic and research settings.* Cambridge: Cambridge University Press

Swannock Fulton, R Storyteller/Writer, Galway: www.storytellersunlimited.com

Wilkinson, J (1971) *The foundations of language.* Oxford University Press

Wray, D and Lewis, M (1997) *Extending literacy: reading and writing non fiction.* London: Routledge

Zipes J (1993) *The trials & tribulations of Little Red Riding Hood,* New York: Routledge

Zipes, J (1995) *Creative storytelling: building community, changing lives.* New York: Routledge

Index